No one has ever accused me or Austin Ruse of seeing the world through rose-colored glasses. But we agree on this: there's no better time than now to be a faithful Catholic. The great temptation is to turn from current troubles and long for the past. But that's not the way of Abraham or Moses or Augustine or Kolbe. Nor is it the way of this book, which offers us a clear path forward.

—Scott Hahn, Father Michael Scanlan TOR Professor of Biblical Theology and the New Evangelization, University of Steubenville

An audacious book by an audacious man of faith.

—Mary Eberstadt, author of *Primal Screams: How the Sexual Revolution Created Identity Politics*

At a time when the Catholic Church faces one of her greatest existential crises, afflicted from within and without, Austin Ruse paradoxically finds hope and strength in *Under Siege*. Societal collapse and the rise of a "woke" paganism that has become, in effect, the new American state religion inspires in him a Christian call to action and a pugnacious return to Church Militant first principles. "Halos are hanging from the lowest branches of the trees," he observes. "Just reach up and grab one."

—Michael Walsh, longtime opera critic for *Time*, author of *Last Stands: Why Men Fight When All Is Lost*

We are living in a religious age. People don't realize that because our new religion is not Christianity but an odd syncretic blend of paganism, sexual polyversity, and scientism that doesn't really have a name. It replaced Christianity so gradually that most people did't notice, but the courts, the media, and the government enforce it more and more strictly. It sows hatred and ruins lives. Austin Ruse describes its rise and our fall clearly, accurately, and powerfully.

—John O'Sullivan, senior fellow at the National Review Institute

Austin Ruse is a courageous and fearless fighter in a culture and country gone barking mad. He has suffered for standing by his beliefs and yet remains an unafraid and cheerful warrior. The self-proclaimed champions of "tolerance" refuse to tolerate him. You can be sure they also will refuse to tolerate or even open this book. That's even more reason for you to get it and see what Austin has to say.

—Paul Kengor, Ph.D., professor of political science, author of *The Devil and Karl Marx*

Austin Ruse has very good news. You and I were not born too soon or too late. We are the spoiled children of Providence and living in the only golden age there will ever be for us. If you've felt dislocated, you'll find your place in these pages. Read up and gain momentum for the years to come.

—Mike Aquilina, author of *How Christianity Saved Civilization . . . and Must Do So Again*

I am by constitution a fighter and a pessimist. But God does not call us to optimism. He calls us to hope and to the actions energized by hope and faith and love. Austin Ruse's book is a call to fight a crazed culture with that good cheer that has already won half the battle and is a reminder that God has placed us here, now, for His purposes, and we are to thank Him for the privilege. On, then!

—Anthony Esolen, author of *Sex and the Unreal City*

I will strongly recommend this great book to all my children, and put it into the hands of every young man and woman I know, as the best guide to where we stand now, and why we are so blessed to be alive in these times.

—Michael Pakaluk, author of *Mary's Voice in the Gospel according to Saint John*, professor of ethics and social philosophy, The Catholic University of America

Looking at the state of the Church, the family, and our country, many Catholics are tempted to retreat, give up, or give in. Some popular Christian writers are advising just that. Austin Ruse has spent decades in the trenches, and he offers a bracing rebuttal to these counsels of decline and despair. The darkness of our moment is an opportunity for the light of the gospel to shine all the brighter! If you're a faithful Catholic who feels like throwing up your hands and surrendering, you need to read this book.

—Jay Richards, author of *The Price of Panic: How the Tyranny of Experts Turned a Pandemic into a Catastrophe*

This book packs a lot of punch with the kind of news our souls long to hear: that God is with us and has selected us to live in these trying times. With Ruse's signature wit, *Under Siege* reveals the good, the bad, and the downright ugly, but offers a fresh vantage point to embrace our challenges with joy and deep confidence in God, come what may.

—Carrie Gress, author of *The Anti-Mary Exposed* and *Theology of Home*

Under Siege

Also by Austin Ruse

As Author

*Littlest Suffering Souls: Children Whose
Short Lives Point Us to Christ*

*Fake Science: Exposing the Left's Skewed Statistics,
Fuzzy Facts, and Dodgy Data*

The Catholic Case for Trump

As Contributor

*Chosen: How Christ Sent Twenty-Three Surprised
Converts to Replant His Vineyard*

Beauty for Ashes: Spiritual Reflections on the Attack on America

Austin Ruse

Under Siege
No Finer Time to Be
a Faithful Catholic

CRISIS
PUBLICATIONS

Manchester, New Hampshire

Crisis Publications
Box 5284, Manchester, NH 03108
1-800-888-9344

www.CrisisMagazine.com

paperback ISBN 978-1-64413-034-6

ebook ISBN 978-1-64413-035-3

Library of Congress Control Number: 2021930527

For three men I read into the Church:

William F. Buckley
Thomas Merton
Anthony Burgess

In your book were written,
every one of them,
the days that were formed for me.

—Psalm 139:16

Contents

Acknowledgments

I don't remember when I first gave the speech "No Finer Time to Be a Faithful Catholic." It was years ago, and what I remember is that every time I have given it, the response has been amazing, people often on their feet cheering.

The central message—that the bad guys have us surrounded and that's just where we want them—somehow resonates in these dark days. That we are living through a time of great saints and spiritual giants is the true food people need right now.

At the annual Catholic Leadership Summit, the idea for a book was first raised by a great and good man, author Mike Aquilina. Mike is a gentleman who has published something on the order of forty books, each beloved by Catholic audiences. He simply said that this has to be a book. First and foremost, I need to thank Mike for his comments that day and his ongoing advice and encouragement, and for reading one of the drafts and making it better.

I gladly thank the excellent people at Sophia Institute Press, a publisher that has meant so much to me over the years. I pitched the idea of this book to Charlie McKinney, Tom Allen, and the legendary Sophia founder and editor John Barger on a sunny day in New Hampshire. They bought the book immediately.

Under Siege

A little more than a year ago, I gave the "Never a Finer Time" speech to a dinner for the Family Institute of Connecticut. Afterward, I met Drew Oliver, a man I have come to admire greatly and who has become a good friend. Drew was the literary editor at *National Review* in his twenties and then went off to make filthy lucre. That evening, Drew expressed a desire to get back on the public-policy hustings. I asked Sophia Institute Press if Drew could edit my book. I gave him a manuscript that, quite frankly, I had lost control of. He put the whole thing in order, moved chapters around, sharpened arguments. In short, Drew made it much better than it was. I am grateful for his deft hand and easy manner.

I want to acknowledge a scholar whose work I did not know but has utterly changed my thinking. Professor Steven D. Smith is a professor of law at the University of San Diego who has written many books and articles about America's founding, the Constitution, and who we are as a people. I am particularly grateful to him for his book *Pagans and Christians in the City: Culture Wars from the Tiber to the Potomac*. It is one of those rare books that changes the way you think and stays with you for a long time. He was very kind with my pestering e-mails over these past months.

I also want to thank several friends and colleagues who read drafts of the book. This was the most challenging book I have written to date, and the subject matter tended in some spots to be out of my area of expertise. Each of them offered wonderful advice and insight. I am particularly grateful for the friendship and guidance of author and thinker Jay Richards. I especially appreciate the light touch of his erudition. Additionally, Michael Pakaluk of the Catholic University of America offered wise advice, as did Matthew Mehan, who is the director of academic programs at Hillsdale College in Washington, D.C. Fr. Larry Kutz, a wise and holy priest, also gave me guidance and counsel, as did my friend Kathleen Abela, who aided me with the chapter on fear. The mistakes that remain are entirely my own.

I owe a great debt of gratitude to my colleagues at C-Fam, Lisa Correnti, Stefano Gennarini, Rebecca Oas, and Hannah Russo. My attention was taken away from our UN mission for many months.

Finally, I want to thank my wife, Cathy, and our children, Lucy and Gigi. It is hard to live with someone buried in a book. I have received only joy and encouragement from this family God somehow gave to me.

Introduction

We live these days in a dark valley. We kill our elderly in the name of compassion. We kill our children in the name of convenience. We mutilate sexual organs in the name of God knows what. We warm ourselves with the cold comfort of believing that at least we seem to be better than the ancient Romans.

In my many years of writing columns and essays, I have spent a lot of time staring into the abyss. I have considered this to be my beat. My wife does similar work, and she often jokes macabrely with me about all the things we have seen in this dark valley. Sometimes we wish we did not know quite so much. As the "replicant" Roy Batty says in *Blade Runner*, "I've seen things you people wouldn't believe."

But this is the work God has given me to do: to look into the abyss and to tell you what I see.

You may think looking into the abyss will change you. It can. It might. I do not recommend it to everyone. Thomas Gray speaks to those who cannot: "Where ignorance is bliss, 'tis folly to be wise." But this book is not about the darkness. It is about the joy, the joy of knowing that God has sent us here, right now, to protect His creation. It is also about courage, sometimes even reckless courage.

Under Siege

There is a scene in the 1987 movie *Full Metal Jacket* where a sniper has pinned down American soldiers in the streets of Hue during the 1968 Tet Offensive. Two men have been shot and are lying in the open, writhing in agony. The platoon leader, "Cowboy," orders his troops to stand down, saying, "We cannot refuse to accept the situation." For years, I had thought his wise admonition was that we must be fearless in knowing and addressing the difficulties before us. But I watched the movie again recently and saw things differently, things that are applicable to our times. Cowboy urges caution because he is afraid of losing more men. His counsel is to hunker down and hide behind the rubble in the street—a tactical retreat. But his fear doesn't help the men who have been shot; neither does it help the men who are with him behind the rubble. It only preserves the snipers in their perch. "Animal Mother," strapped with ammo and toting a massive machine gun, refuses to accept the situation. He ignores Cowboy, jumps over the rubble, and charges forward, machine gun blazing. He understands the situation, but he refuses to "accept" it. Though he cannot rescue the dying men, he does rally the troops, who in short order take out the sniper. In one final, sad irony, it is not Animal Mother who gets killed by the sniper's bullet, but Cowboy.

Heroes are those who confront evil and charge the sniper's nest. That is the situation we are in.

In His great providence, God has allowed a great evil to come upon our land. But He has also sent us, in His great providence, to do something about it. What an honor that is, an honor that we should accept. We should not accept that the situation is lost; we should not hunker down and wait for better days. We are the Lord's hands and feet on this earth, and better days rely upon us. We must charge the sniper's nests now lodged in the government, the academy, the corporations, the media, Hollywood. We must charge with joy in our hearts that this is the mission that He gave to us.

Come with me through the valley of the shadow of death, for not only is He with us: He sent us! And on the other side is sunlight and great joy.

In chapter 1, we descend into the abyss. Some of what we see will be known to you; some will be new. All of it is horrifying. But never fear; the chapter is not explicit. It is intended only to show accurately the landscape that we are in, so we can think about it clearly.

In chapter 2, I explain how we ended up in this dreadful place. It was not simply bad luck or bad fate. Powerful people set us down this path. I take a closer look at the wall of separation between church and state. This wall has been breached, but not in the way the liberal media says it has been breached. Indeed, it has been breached by the government on behalf of new faiths. Did you think we live in a pluralistic society where each faith is equal before a neutral and benevolent government? We don't. In fact, I argue that there is a rising State Church with dogmas enforced by local, state, and federal governments, along with allies in the academy, the media, and corporate America.

In chapter 3, we further examine how this new State Church functions. We discover who are its priests and prophets, and what is its mission. We also look at the celebrated "nones" who have largely drifted away from Christianity. In fact, these nones are not nothing. They are deeply religious, and in many ways, they have helped form the denominations of the new State Church. They consider Christians to be the new heretics, and they treat us accordingly.

In chapters 4 and 5, I describe our situation in its historical context. You will be surprised at how our current fight is quite ancient and how it is playing out in the same way it did a few thousand years ago. Oddly, this should give us some comfort. We have already fought these same battles—and won.

In chapter 6, after we have really explored and understood the situation we are in, I look at attitudes that tempt Catholics: living frozen in fear, living lost in nostalgic fantasies, or dissipating our days in distractions, sports, video games, and much else. In this chapter, I admonish you not to miss the great mission that our Father has sent us on.

But finally, the joy. In chapter 7, I demonstrate how we are living through one of the most remarkable epochs the Church has ever known, and I implore you to see that never has there been a finer time to be a faithful Catholic. I urge my fellow Catholics and all Christians not to miss this extraordinary time. Our descendants will envy it just as we envy the time of our founding generation, the generation of the Civil War, and the Greatest Generation. This is what awaits us if we embrace the job God sent us to do.

For the last several years, I have been giving a talk to audiences around the country called "No Finer Time to Be a Faithful Catholic." It is always met with cheers and standing ovations. With so much evil around us, and for so long, people tend to forget what an astonishing time we are living through—not in spite of the troubles all around us, but precisely because of the troubles. We were made for union with God in Heaven. But on this earth, we were made for fighting.

Austin Ruse
October 22, 2020
Feast of Pope St. John Paul the Great

I Am Lazarus Come from the Dead, Come Back to Tell You All

We are deep into a civilizational abyss. But you must not look away from the evil that clings to its walls. You have to look. You cannot fight back if you blind yourself to our national nightmare. But do not abandon hope as we begin our descent into this fetid cavern. Remember to be of good cheer. The good Lord Himself placed us here, right now. He knows what He is about.

"Transgenderism"

Let us begin with "transgenderism." This is without a doubt one of the most disturbing and vile developments in our society. It is an idea based on a pillar of lies, lies even more vicious than homosexualism. At its base, the idea is that God or nature made a mistake with some people and gave them the wrong reproductive organs. But on top of that is piled the assertion that the failure is not actually God's, or nature's, but rather ours for failing to perceive this unusual color of the rainbow. After that, truth itself is assaulted with the diabolical claim that if a man with male parts says he is female, ergo females must be able to have penises; 2 + 2 = 5. The capstone of the idea is that really there is no God, at least no Christian God, and so the meaning of the world, or gender, or sex, or anything, is whatever we want — and whoever is strongest gets to make everyone else accept their meaning, because in a world without God, might makes right. Oh yes, at least politically speaking, "transgenderism" is very much about power. Scary, right?[1]

"Transgenderism" began on the far fringes of society, in the deep crevasses of psychosexual depravity. Some disturbed men really did believe they were women; and some women really did believe they were men. In New York and San Francisco, a small fetishistic community of cross-dressing drag queens sashayed about in dresses, clownishly aping women. To them, women were strippers or prostitutes, so they mostly made a mockery of the fair sex. Their antics were akin to black-face and the old vaudeville routines in which white men cavorted in the crude ways they supposed black men and women might.

Though entirely different, it was not as if men in dresses were unknown to mainstream audiences. Famed movie stars and television personalities dressed like women for a laugh. In the 1950s, Milton Berle's character Aunt Mildred made television audiences howl. Johnny Carson entertained his crowds with his character Aunt Blabby. Tony Curtis and Jack Lemmon dressed as women to hide from gangsters in the movie *Some Like It Hot*. Tom Hanks starred in a television program called *Bosom Buddies*, in which he and a friend dressed like women so they could live in a women's hotel in New York because New York apartments

---

[1] This idea is essentially Justice Anthony Kennedy's idea of the world: "At the heart of liberty is the right to define one's own concept of existence, of meaning, of the universe, and of the mystery of human life" (Planned Parenthood v. Casey, 505 U.S. 833). But we will get to that soon enough.

were so expensive. All of these were played for laughs. And we did laugh.

But with the inevitable depravity of the sexual revolution, along with the hubris of modern medicine and psychiatry, grew the credentialed notion that men who thought they were women, or women who thought they were men, were not simply nuts but were experiencing certifiable gender dysphoria, eventually "gender identity disorder"—in which case, it could be treated with combinations of drugs and surgery, for a fee. In other words, a potent combination of disturbed patients, ideologically crazed "gender counselors," and medical doctors eager to try out their new powers validated subjective descriptions of reality rather than the reality presented by their patient's physical bodies, and a trail of sad, mutilated people followed. So much for science.

All this may have given a slight titillation to the masses, a chuckle, an eye roll. A "wonder what the world's coming to" on a comedy show. But then it metastasized, and it was no longer funny.

In my 2017 book *Fake Science*, I reported that in 1995, "the *New York Times* published a grand total of 2 mentions of the word 'transgender' and one was not a news story but a letter to the editor. The other was about a gay pride parade in San Francisco." Five years later, the paper of record mentioned "transgender" 24 times, almost all of them within the context of the ubiquitous acronym LGBT. Five years later, there were 54 mentions. In 2010, there were 190. After that, the deluge. In 2015, the Supreme Court imposed same-sex "marriage" on the country through the *Obergefell* decision, and the *New York Times* mentioned "transgender" 752 times. A year later, 1,166 times. That is an average of three stories per day every day of the year.

Under Siege

It was predictable that the elites who had imposed homosexual "marriage" on the country through the courts would not permit Americans to turn their attention elsewhere, not even after gays had been given all they said they wanted. The LGBT power centers could not simply disband. Their issue had to be kept hot. They started making it about the kids. Most transgender "women"—that is, men in dresses—look a lot like Corporal Max Klinger from the old TV show M*A*S*H. Corporal Klinger was aiming for a "Section 8" psychological exit from military service, so he always dressed like a woman. It was a great joke because Klinger looked nothing like a woman. He was hairy from top to toe with a huge Adam's apple, which is what most transgender "women" look like. But a nine-year-old boy can quite easily look like a nine-year-old girl. And who wants to criticize a child? So the ideologues pushed the kids to the front.

One of the first and most famous of these children, pushed into the limelight in 2006, was a boy named Jaron Seth Bloshinsky, now known as "Jazz Jennings." When he was a toddler, his mother noticed that he liked to unsnap his onesie. She said this made her believe that he considered himself a girl and that he was signaling this by creating a skirt. Really. She consulted a "gender specialist" who, for a fee, dutifully echoed the mother's opinion and recommended a regimen of untested drugs that would interrupt Jaron's puberty process, prevent his scrotum from developing, and prepare his body to be pumped full of estrogen and grow breasts. As he matured, "Jazz" progressed from drugs to physical butchery by unscrupulous doctors who castrated him, cut away the top of his penis, and folded it into a bleeding wound that may never fully heal. They erroneously call this excavation a vagina.

This is all grotesque, but bearded ladies have always attracted a circus of attention. "Jazz" eventually wrote a book, starred in a reality TV show, and appeared on *Oprah*.

Note that when "Jazz" was young, he did pass quite well as a little girl. As he ages, however, he has come to look more like Corporal Klinger, and his sad story is unlikely ever to have a happy ending. Many like him commit suicide. But you must only cheer "Jazz Jennings." Any criticism is considered hatred and bigotry by our social elites.

Consider a young woman whose story was told by Ryan Anderson in his book *When Harry Became Sally*. She wanted to be a man, and so she started on testosterone gel at age eighteen and soon switched to injections. It was not long before her voice broke, her hips narrowed, and her shoulders broadened. She had her healthy breasts amputated in an operation that has left her with severe scarring. The young woman now says, "I am a female who looks like a man. I will always have a broken voice and will never grow breasts." She never received any counseling to try to understand the underlying issues that made her feel like a boy. But according to researchers, almost all confused young people, if they are left alone, eventually work out their confusion and become happy with the sex and the body they were born with.[2]

But this does not happen if they meet the wrong kind of "helpers." On a transgender YouTube channel, a young woman named Cari describes her experience. She "transitioned" to become a

[2] Kenneth J. Zucker, "The Myth of Persistence: Response to 'A Critical Commentary on Follow-Up Studies and "Desistance" Theories about Transgender and Gender Non-Conforming Children,'" *International Journal of Transgenderism* 19, no. 2 (May 2018): 231–245, Taylor & Francis Online, https://www.tandfonline.com/doi/full/10.1080/15532739.2018.1468293.

"boy" at age fifteen, first by taking hormones and then by having her breasts cut off. Then she de-transitioned, to the extent possible, at twenty-two. "When I was transitioning," she says, "no one in the medical or psychological field ever tried to dissuade me, to offer other options, to do really anything to stop me." Instead, she was given testosterone after only three or four visits to the gender counselor.

There is increasing research that shows that those on the autism spectrum have an unusually high propensity for gender confusion.[3] They are easy marks for an ideologically driven industry with plenty of pills and surgical procedures. On Breitbart four years ago, I told the story of a left-wing academic at the University of Michigan who was trying to rescue her autistic daughter from the clutches of gender ideologists.[4] Dr. Kathleen Levinstein says her daughter, who has the functional age of nine, was given massive testosterone injections because she believed the drugs would allow her to "grow a penis." Such was her separation from reality. Levinstein told me at the time, "My daughter was wholly unprepared to make these decisions." But her daughter's breasts were cut off anyway. Dr. Levinstein correctly calls this "medical torture."

---

[3] Anglia Ruskin University, "Study Finds Transgender, Non-Binary Autism Link," Medical Xpress, July 16, 2019, https://medicalxpress.com/news/2019-07-transgender-non-binary-autism-link.html; "Gender Identity and Autism," Autism Speaks, June 28, 2019, https://www.autismspeaks.org/expert-opinion/gender-identity-and-autism; Bryony White, "The Link Between Autism and Trans Identity," *Atlantic*, November 15, 2016, https://www.theatlantic.com/health/archive/2016/11/the-link-between-autism-and-trans-identity/507509/.

[4] Levinstein said she legally emancipated her daughter before legal adulthood because she feared her daughter would be institutionalized if Levinstein died.

Doctors and parents are also concerned about "social contagion"—that is, the sudden and spontaneous development of
gender dysphoria among a group of girls with no prior indicators
of dysphoria. A study from Brown University examined "rapid
onset gender dysphoria" and concluded that groups of friends
who watched certain YouTube channels on "transgenderism"
would become "transgender" *en masse*, and almost immediately.
The study has since been withdrawn by Brown after "Brown
Community members expressed concerns that the conclusions of
the study could be used to discredit efforts to support transgender
youth and invalidate the perspectives of members of the transgender community." It should be recalled that Brown University
installed tampon machines in men's bathrooms because "not all
people who menstruate are women."

If you think that "transgenderism" has happened ferociously
fast, you are right. The first gender clinic in the United States
opened in Boston in 2007. As of 2016, there were more than
sixty. Some states now provide taxpayer-funded "sex changes"
for children as young as fifteen, without parental approval or
even notification.[5] Lawmakers in Oregon have ensured that
the surgeons who mutilate these children are protected from
liability.

On the other hand, doctors who urge caution are hounded
from the industry. Dr. Kenneth Zucker ran a highly respected
clinic in Canada that dealt with gender dysphoria. In treating
a patient, he would try to understand the underlying reasons

[5] Dan Springer, "Oregon Allowing 15-Year-Olds to Get State-
Subsidized Sex-Change Operations," Fox News, last updated
May 2, 2016, https://www.foxnews.com/politics/oregon-allowing
-15-year-olds-to-get-state-subsidized-sex-change-operations.

for the dysphoria and consider how the patient might become comfortable with his or her birth sex. He argued for what he calls "watchful waiting," following the data that shows that gender confusion will almost inevitably work itself out. Because of his heterodox view, he was forced out of his own clinic. He did eventually receive an apology and a cash settlement for libel. But now the law is beginning to turn.

Brandon Showalter of *Christianity Post* has told the story of an eight-year-old boy who informed his grandmother one day that his name was not Jack but Jacquelyn. The boy's father was not married to his mother. His mother became a lesbian and took up with another woman, whom she married. Her lesbian "spouse" then came out as transgender and started using a male name. It was then that the boy was identified by his mom as transgender. The poor boy's grandmother was informed that if she did not go along with "Jacquelyn's" new identity, she would be written out of his life. The grandmother tried to get Child Protective Services to consider that her grandson is experiencing child abuse, but governmental bodies are becoming enforcers of the new orthodoxy and punishers of heresy, and so the government refused. The grandmother says she cries herself to sleep most nights.

Consider the case of six-year-old James Younger, who is being forced by his mother to wear dresses as a girl named Luna. When he is with his dad, James is all boy. He chooses boy clothes and boy toys. But the mother has custody, and so James is being pushed toward puberty blockers, cross-sex hormones, and perhaps surgery. The boy's father went to court to fight what was happening to his son. The court sided with the mother. Now the father is required by court directive to refer to his son as a daughter and to use his female name and pronouns. If he refuses, he will lose all contact with his son.

You've likely heard that "transgender boys" are being allowed to participate in athletics with real girls. These transmogrified "girls" are winning the awards and often the college athletic scholarships, as real girls are left high and dry. This is perfectly fine with the governing body of these schools and athletic conferences. But when the Alliance Defending Freedom (ADF) brought a lawsuit in Connecticut on behalf of real girl athletes to ensure that they have to compete only against other girls, the judge told the ADF attorneys they could not refer to these male athletes as "male." He said, "I'm not asking you to refer to these individuals as 'females.' I know that you don't want to do so. What I'm saying is you must refer to them as 'transgender females' rather than as 'males.' Again, that's the more accurate terminology, and I think that it fully protects your clients' legitimate interests. Referring to these individuals as 'transgender females' is consistent with science, common practice and perhaps human decency. To refer to them as 'males,' period, is not accurate, certainly not as accurate, and I think it's needlessly provocative."[6] Is there any way this judge can be expected to rule impartially in this case? He has accepted the transgender ideology, and the complaint of the real girls is mystifying to him.

Child Pornography

So much of the darkness upon our land has to do with attacks upon or exploitation of children. It seems the Old Testament

[6]   David Fowler, "Alice in Wonderland Meets Judge Humpty Dumpty in 'Transgender' Lawsuit," Family Action Council of Tennessee, May 15, 2020, https://www.factennessee.org/news-views/commentary/2020/alice-in-wonderland-meets-judge-humpty-dumpty-in-transgender-lawsuit.

god Moloch, who demanded child sacrifice, is alive and well in our times. Besides abortion, there is no higher altar to Moloch than the abuse of children in pornography.

One of the most serious problems for those trying to combat evil is the natural inclination of normal people to look away from it, to avoid looking into the abyss. I do not recommend looking at child pornography. But we must know about it, and some, quite frankly, have to look. The U.S. Congress did not move against child porn until anti-porn activists took around a booklet of actual pictures. Once Congress saw, they acted. Our enemies count on our not looking. Our enemies count on our looking away. One of the themes of this book is that we must look. We must know what is in the filthy pools where our children are drowning. It may be repugnant, but God commands us to see.

Child porn is one of the fastest-growing businesses on the Internet. Some estimate its annual revenues to be three billion dollars, though the real numbers are unknown because the rapid growth of cryptocurrency hides the money trail. The Association of Sites Advocating Child Protection estimates that the United States hosts the largest share of commercial child-porn sites, upwards of 50 percent of the global total.

Still, the law does catch up with the criminals, sometimes. In the fall and winter of 2019, after a years-long investigation into the sexual exploitation of minors, Toronto police rescued 400 children and arrested 347 adults. More than 100 Canadians were arrested along with 76 Americans, and another 164 from around the world. Called Project Spade, the investigation began when Toronto police discovered a man sharing graphic sexual images of children. A movie production company run by forty-two-year-old Brian Way was discovered operating on the Web. Investigators found hundreds of thousands of images and videos of the most monstrous kind, forty-five terabytes of data with an estimated worth of millions of dollars.

In another case, the U.S. Department of Justice arrested the South Korean operator of the world's "largest dark web child porn marketplace." Joo Woo Son, only twenty-three, was charged with nine counts, including one count of advertising child porn, two counts of distribution, and three counts of money laundering. The Justice Department rounded up 337 suspects in thirty-eight countries, including 23 in the United States. Forensic experts say that Woo's cache of child porn included 250,000 unique videos and that 45 percent of the videos included images not previously known to exist. Twenty-three minors in the United States, the United Kingdom, and Spain who were being actively abused were rescued.

Are we still able to be shocked about this, shocked that many of those arrested were in regular contact with children and were in highly respected professions; that they were nurses, teachers, doctors, policemen, pastors, and even priests? There is a chance someone in your own neighborhood is eyeing the most horrific images of child sexual abuse. Experts estimate that Americans are among the hungriest consumers of this filth.

According to the Crimes Against Children Research Center, those who share child-porn images, so-called peer-to-peer users, are more likely to have younger and younger images. Among those arrested in 2009, 33 percent possessed images of toddlers aged three and younger. Forty-two percent had images of children showing sexual violence.

How is this happening? Moloch's lust for child flesh aside, there are multiple reasons regular people succumb to this nauseating temptation. First, the vast increase in easily and anonymously accessible adult pornography, which I will discuss further below, has ensnared a generation of porn users. Thirty years ago, they might have had to put themselves in physical danger to acquire pictures. It is so easy now. The Internet is a child's game. Furthermore, porn users, like drug abusers, require more and stronger doses to get the same stimulation that tamer images once provided. So the images must get nastier and, in many cases, younger.

But in addition, children are being sexualized by society, not only by the culture, but by the very people to whom they are entrusted on a daily basis: their own teachers. Sex-ed has become practically pornographic. This both arouses children's curiosity and turns them into sexualized creatures.

The Fairfax County School Board in suburban Washington, D.C., requires children as young as five to receive explicit sex education. At the tenderest of ages, they are given instruction in oral sex. By the time they are fourteen, according to a curriculum that parents cannot readily see, they are taught about anal sex. Twenty-two times they are told about anal sex. This is nothing less than grooming, preparing children to act out sexually.

Pediatrician and outspoken child advocate Michelle Cretella tells the story of a little girl who had been subjected to a male classmate's "coming out" ceremony as a "trans girl" that had been orchestrated by the teacher, without the parents' knowledge. One night, getting out of the bathtub and seeing her own long hair slicked back, the little girl burst into tears and asked her mother if she was turning into a boy.

In all likelihood, you have no idea what is happening in the public school right down the street from where you live. You certainly do not know what is happening in the school down the street from my house in Fairfax County, Virginia. I will use Fairfax County Schools as an example because no less than Gay, Lesbian, Straight Education Network (GSLEN), a radical homosexual group, has proudly announced that our schools are a laboratory for the rest of the country. It is the tenth-largest school district in the county, located only a few miles from the Department of Education in Washington, D.C.

We first noticed the radicalism of our local school board — which is led by a homosexual who used to be an official in the Obama administration — when it voted ten to one to let boys into the girls' bathrooms and showers. The board claimed it was necessary to stop bullying, though a Freedom of Information Act request showed there had not been even a single complaint about "trans" bullying. This decision, made without hearings, impact studies, or public engagement, unleashed a torrent of opposition from moms and dads who began appearing at the biweekly school-board meetings practically begging the school board to reverse the policy. But the homosexual chairman of the board threatened to have them removed, saying they were "on the wrong side of history."

As my wife has written, the policy was not about bullying. It was about forcing all children and families to change their behaviors, their speech, and ultimately their beliefs, to conform to the new government-mandated orthodoxy. And this is one of the main themes of this book. We are facing a new religious orthodoxy, one imposed by the government.

The Fairfax County School students are government-monitored laboratory rats for other forms of social and sexual experimentation. Sex ed is now called Family Life Education, though family, of course, is never even mentioned in the curriculum. The only mention of fathers was a video about a father raping his daughter. Neither do they mention male or female, only "sex assigned at birth." They promote among ninth graders a daily gay sex drug called PrEP, which is supposed to ward off HIV infection, thus enabling gay men to have all the gay sex they want. Yes, they are pushing this on kids.

All told, our local school board requires children to experience eighty hours of sex ed. Sixth graders get lessons about "sex partners." Seventh graders get more lessons on "anal sex." Eighth graders are subjected to twenty-two references to "anal sex" and twenty references to "oral sex." Tenth graders get lessons promoting abortion and about how to get one without telling their parents. Of course, they do mention abstinence, by which they mean abstaining from sex between "faithful monogamous relationships." So much for marriage.

Can parents opt their children out? For now. But they have to know what is going on, and the schools make that as hard as possible. Materials are never sent home. Parents must hunt through hundreds of pages of online material. And if an engaged mom or dad opts a child out, that child is embarrassed, even harassed, for being taken out of class. Yes, this is what provokes the real bullying. But even that might not work anymore: much of this material is being shunted into other classes. Kids get "trans" stuff in history now, and literature, and all the other disciplines. There is nowhere to hide.

But the revolting sexual indoctrination is only part of the darkness. The schools are also teaching your kids to hate Christianity and their own country. In their book *Get Out Now: Why You Should Pull Your Child from Public School Before It's Too Late*, Mary Rice Hasson and Theresa Farnan tell the story of James Corbett, a California science teacher who was fond of attacking Christianity in the classroom. He told the kids that putting on "Jesus glasses" would blind Christians to scientific truth. He told them that believing in God was as ridiculous as believing in a "gigantic spaghetti monster living behind the moon." Fed-up parents finally took the case to court and were told by a judge that his classroom behavior was "appropriate and legitimate." Where Christian virtues and love of country were once taught in our schools, now a new religion has official sanction. There is very little parents can do about it.

As for anti-Americanism, there has been no more influential history book in our time than Howard Zinn's A *People's History of the United States.* It is a primer for hating America, and you can be sure that most of those who teach history to kids have been steeped deeply in Zinn. But there are plenty of other offensive books. Hassan and Farnan point to the National Network of State Teachers of the Year, which recommended a smelly book called the *Social Justice Book List.* It lists the themes of "classism, racism, xenophobia, sexism, and transgenderism." This is for kids in preschool through sixth grade. If you wonder why your fourth grader comes home sounding like Jeremiah Wright, this is why.

Children are groomed in school. Did you know they are also groomed through video games? NoFap, a growing secular organization of young men fighting what used to be called self-abuse (masturbation) reported on a popular game distribution platform called Steam that sells a game called "Porno Studio Tycoon." You have probably never heard of Steam, but it boasts 125 million accounts with nearly 30 percent of its users under the age of eighteen.

NoFap found a Steam game called House Party, the purpose of which is to "get laid." House Party features "animated pornography" where a player has a first-person view. He can virtually pull out his penis, get women drunk, and receive oral and penetrative sex from partygoers. During penetrative sex, where the genitals and the women's breasts are fully visible and bouncing, an orgasm-meter gradually fills up until the players ejaculate on the faces or bodies of the women.

That this is a game for kids is horrifying enough. But worse, it breaks down barriers that can be easily exploited by adults who prey upon children—including credentialed academics. There is now an active pressure group among individuals and even academics to regularize pedophilia as simply another form of sexual orientation and expression. Only a few decades ago, the homosexual Man-Boy Love Association was driven underground. No longer.

Pat Fagan of the Catholic University of America reminds us that Christian children were once kidnapped by the sultan and turned into an elite army called Janissaries whose job it was to destroy Christian communities. In much the same way, Christian children today are being trained, mostly in school, specifically to wage war upon the Christian beliefs and practices of their parents. This is happening not just in college but even in grade school.

Let us move beyond what they are doing to children to what they are doing to adults.

Adult Pornography

According to the U.S. Centers for Disease Control, young unmarried adults in Gen Z are having less sex than millennials, Xers, or boomers. At first blush, this sounds like good news. Maybe the kids have wised up? Perhaps abstinence education has finally kicked in? Maybe they've seen the damage done to their older brothers and sisters and even their parents? Perhaps. But it may be something else.

Jon Ronson produced a seven-part podcast series called *The Butterfly Effect* that explored what happened when the world was given free pornography through the "genius" of a young man named Fabian Thylmann. Thylmann revolutionized the world of pornography and became fabulously wealthy in the process.

Before we get to Thylmann, who is arguably the Sam Walton of porn, consider the widely recognized understanding that frequent use of pornography makes it increasingly difficult for the consumer to relate to real human beings. Even married men and women find a lessened interest in sex with their spouses when they are regular users of pornography. Documentarian Ronson says this has had an impact on teens as well as adults. He points out that erectile-dysfunction rates have grown tenfold among young men since the rise of free porn. That's right, our kids are watching so much free porn that it has blunted their interest in real sexual relations. We may applaud the result, but the cause is reason for profound concern.

It is important to point out that this pro-porn documentarian is not the only one who makes this case. So did the largely conservative scholars who produced the magisterial *Social Costs of Pornography* ten years ago. The attendant paper was written by social conservative scholar and hero Mary Eberstadt.

Here is what happened. This is why some people, including young adults, are losing their interest in sexual relations.

It is commonplace knowledge that porn exploded onto the newly born Internet. Prior to the Internet, porn was available only to those willing to embarrass themselves by asking for *Playboy* down at the 7-Eleven or those willing to trudge to the smutty part of town.

Then came the Internet, and anyone could log onto a smutty site. Porn producers in the San Fernando Valley were fat and happy. But you still had to pay to enter because the typical porn site had links that you had to pay to access. You couldn't see anything unless you paid. This was still a barrier for use, and especially a barrier for kids.

But then, three foosball fanatics in Montreal and a computer nerd in Belgium changed all that. It started with the YouTube revolution in 2005. YouTube allowed anyone to upload his own videos or pirated videos of others. While the foosball trio in Montreal had traditional porn sites with paid links, it occurred to them to put up free porn on so-called Tubes. Free porn turned into a contagion. You could watch hours of porn and never pay a dime. This changed the world of pornography so fast that the hard-core-porn producers in the San Fernando Valley did not know what hit them. And neither did society. How did the trio make money? Through advertising worth hundreds of millions of dollars. And all while the world got hooked.

The company was originally called Mansef, then Manwin. It is now called MindGeek. Few have heard of it, but MindGeek is not only the largest porn company in the world by far; it outstrips Facebook and Google for consumer engagements. You read that right. You have surely heard about Mark Zuckerberg (Facebook) and Jeff Bezos (Amazon) and Sergey Brin (Google), but you have probably never heard of Fabian Thylmann or Stephane Manos or Ouissam Youssef or Matt Keezer. These are the fabulously wealthy young men who hooked your friends, or your family, on free porn.

Consider this. In July 2019, Jeff Bezos's Amazon garnered 2.65 billion visits. That's roughly 83 million a day and translates into roughly 31 billion visits a year. The MindGeek family of websites receives 125 million visits per day. That translates into roughly 45 billion per year. MindGeek revenues are estimated to be as high as $97 billion. Compare this with Netflix's $11.7 billion. In 2017, just one of MindGeek's websites transmitted more data than the entire contents of the New York Public Library's fifty million books. MindGeek's bandwidth eclipses both Facebook and Amazon.

Now consider what is being transmitted to the smartphones of kids on playgrounds across America. Much of it is based on violent rape. Most of it is unnatural. Every bit of it is prosecutable under federal law. And it is being hotwired into the minds of adults and children everywhere.

Writing in the *New York Times* in 2018, Maggie Jones tells the story of an eight-year-old boy named Drew who was "flipping through the TV channels at home and landed on 'Girls Gone Wild.'" Sometime later, he came across so-called soft-core porn on HBO. The shows gave him ideas of what real-world sex was supposed to be: buff men sexually dominating submissive women. He recalled specifically one scene where "a woman was bored by a man who approached sex gently but became ecstatic with a far more aggressive guy."

How does this kind of thing affect boys and girls? In the fall of 2019, the BBC reported the rise of young women being choked and slapped during sex. Anna, twenty-three, reported instances of slapping, hair pulling, and even choking. A research company asked 2,002 women between the ages of eighteen and thirty-nine if they had experienced "slapping, choking, gagging, or spitting during consensual sex, and if it was ever unwanted." "More than a third (38%) had experienced these acts and said they *were unwanted at least some of the time*." Note that last part. It suggests that these horrific acts were wanted at least some of the time. This is what pornography teaches consumers.

Data show that 90 percent of men in college and 30 percent of women have watched porn in the previous year. And they are seeing it at younger and younger ages. According to a study by the University of New Hampshire, 93 percent of males and

62 percent of females in college reported having seen porn as adolescents. The average age at which children see porn online for the first time is thirteen for boys and fourteen for girls.

Most parents don't know this. According to research from the University of Indiana, twice as many teenagers watched porn as their parents assumed.[7] Parents also do not know the kind of porn their children consume. Roughly a third of boys and 12 percent of girls had seen gang bangs or rough oral sex.

This has a deep effect on the sexual behavior of boys and girls. According to the Indiana survey, of those who were sexually active, about one-sixth of boys said they had ejaculated onto the face of a girl or choked her during sex. They also participated in the unnatural sex acts they had seen in porn. According to a study published in the *Journal of Sexual Medicine*, the percentage of women aged eighteen to twenty-four who tried anal sex grew from 16 percent in 1992 to 40 percent in 2009. Note this is only three years after the advent of free porn by MindGeek and others. The same survey found that 20 percent of eighteen- and nineteen-year-old women had tried anal sex with roughly 6 percent of fourteen- to seventeen-year-olds having tried it.

MindGeek keeps a massive database of consumer preference and interest. They have more consumer data than any other e-commerce site, including Facebook, Amazon, and Netflix. They use it algorithmically in order to customize porn to particular tastes. It is not known if the data has been used in any other ways. They say that because of the need for consumer privacy,

---

[7] Maggie Jones, "What Teenagers Are Learning from Online Porn," *New York Times*, February 7, 2018. https://www.nytimes.com/2018/02/07/magazine/teenagers-learning-online-porn-literacy-sex-education.html.

they do not share it the way Facebook and others do. However, MindGeek has been willing to enter the political fray with their data. When the South Carolina legislature was considering a so-called bathroom bill that would have kept men out of women's bathrooms, MindGeek released data showing the massive numbers of South Carolinians interested in transgender pornography. This portends ill for any future porn prosecution that relies on community standards.

Abortion

As we continue our tour of the abyss, we must consider abortion. This is perhaps the darkest place we will look at in this dark world. Moloch shows himself here in the deliberate killing of human children.

There is some good news in the American abortion debate. When *Roe v. Wade* was decided by the Supreme Court in 1973, the *New York Times* announced that the issue had been settled. Five decades later, there is no more unsettled issue than this. Twenty years ago, only 35 percent of Americans self-identified as pro-life. Now, the number of Americans who self-identify as pro-life equals those who identify as pro-choice.

Recent figures from the CDC suggest that the number of abortions is down to fewer than seven hundred thousand per year in the United States, though this data is incomplete because California, a large state with presumably a large number of abortions, does not report. The increasing number of chemical, do-it-yourself abortions at home on the toilet are also unreported.

In recent years, more than two hundred bills of pro-life legislation have been passed by state legislatures across the country. These bills require abortion clinics to meet the standards of surgery centers or require abortion doctors to have privileges at the local hospital, something abortionists have a hard time getting. The effect has been to close abortion clinics. Some states are down to only a single abortion clinic.

Unfortunately, these advances probably account for a frightening backlash, a marked increase in abortion radicalism. Early in 2019, the New York State legislature overwhelmingly passed something called the Reproductive Health Act, perhaps the most radical abortion bill ever passed in the United States or anywhere in the world. The bill allows nonmedical personnel to perform abortions. It allows abortion up to the moment of birth. The bill removes protections for children who may survive an abortion. The bill says an unborn child cannot be the victim of a homicide; that is, if the mother is murdered, there is no additional liability for the death of the child. When this bill passed, the New York State legislators stood and cheered. It was gruesome.

Within days, the legislature of the Commonwealth of Virginia passed something similar: a forty-week abortion bill that permitted abortion up to the moment of birth. Quite remarkably, Virginia governor Ralph Northam admitted on radio that it would allow a child to die even if she survives abortion. He said, "If a mother is in labor, I can tell you exactly what would happen. The infant would be delivered. The infant would be kept comfortable. The infant would be resuscitated if that's what the mother and the family desired, and then a discussion would ensue between the physicians and the mother."[8] His position is

---

[8]   Jessica Chasmar, "Ralph Northam, Virginia Governor, Defends Bill Allowing Abortion during Labor," AP News, January 30, 2019, https://apnews.com/article/a5a1456c866b6cd60 d11bb2369b3fdfc.

strikingly similar to the practice in ancient Rome of abandoning newborns in order to kill them.

Indeed, the measure of abortion radicalism is clearly expressed by Democratic legislator Kathy Tran. When asked if her bill would allow abortion at the moment of birth, she replied without fear or embarrassment, "My bill would allow that, yes."[9] This is the brazen nature of today's abortion radicalism.

The radical change among abortion advocates is striking. Not long ago, even among abortion advocates, abortion was supposed to be safe, legal, and rare. Now abortion is promoted as a positive good that should be celebrated. It is as if abortion has become one of the chief sacraments of a new religion.

In November 2019, the National Women's Law Center launched the "Abortion Actually" campaign, intended to reframe the abortion debate. They argue that abortion is "an act of love, an act of compassion, an act of healing, an act of selflessness." Shout Your Abortion is an organization[10] that celebrates abortion stories with headlines such as "I Had an Abortion and It Wasn't Scary, It Was Empowering" and that offers "Abortion is Normal" T-shirts. Singer Miley Cyrus celebrated abortion on Twitter with a photo of her licking a birthday cake that said, "Abortion is Healthcare." Academic David Grimes told the *Los Angeles Times*, "Abortion is good for you, your family and society. It's a win-win-win."[11] Feminist Katha Pollitt wrote, "We need to see abortion as an urgent practical decision that is just as moral

---

[9] Ibid.

[10] Shout Your Abortion, https://shoutyourabortion.com/.

[11] Quoted in Jarrett Stepman, "Why the Pro-Life Movement Is a True Expression of America's Founding Principles," *Daily Signal*, January 19, 2018, https://www.dailysignal.com/2018/01/19/pro-life-movement-true-expression-americas-founding-principles/.

as the decision to have a child—indeed, sometimes more moral. I want us to start thinking of abortion as a positive social good and saying this out loud."[12]

Attacks against pro-life demonstrators have also become increasingly brazen. There are dozens of videos on YouTube showing crazed abortion supporters physically attacking pro-life demonstrators. They tear down signs or steal them. One man kicked a pro-life woman in the face. A teacher screamed obscenities at a student holding a pro-life poster. A Pennsylvania state legislator filmed himself harassing an older lady who was simply praying the Rosary in front of a Philadelphia abortion clinic. He filmed himself harassing two minor girls doing the same thing. He asked his viewers to dox the girls to encourage further harassment.

And what about the sensible restrictions on abortion mentioned above? They are routinely stopped by the courts. Remember the law in Texas that required abortion clinics to have the same standards as outpatient surgery centers and abortionists to have admitting privileges at the local hospital? It was struck down by the courts as impinging upon the right to abortion.

Abortion has become a sacrament in the new orthodoxy, and upwards of a million defenseless babies are killed each and every year in America. Even with all our victories, there is nothing darker than this.

Church

Finally, the darkness in the Church itself must not be overlooked or ignored. The attacks on young men, mostly, by a protected

---

[12] Katha Pollitt, *Pro: Reclaiming Abortion Rights* (New York: Picador, 2014), 16.

class of sexual actors, and their subsequent protection by our Shepherds, has done more damage to our Church than we can imagine. Even here, I blanch at the catalogue of abuses, the hundreds of cases of homosexual predation perpetrated on young men and boys, and some girls. If you have read the details, you know the satanic nature of the crisis; you have read about the ritualistic torture of young men, young men passed around from priest to sick priest.

The Church is paying hundreds of millions, perhaps billions, of dollars to the victims of this homosexual predation. Churches and Catholic schools are being forced to close. States are changing laws so that statutes of limitations no longer protect the Church from decades-old claims. In December 2019, the Associated Press reported on a lawyer named Adam Slater who is beating the hedgerows looking for new clients who may take up to four billion dollars in additional funds from the Church.

There is a photo of Slater staring down from his office at St. Patrick's Cathedral in New York City, asking, "I wonder how much that's worth." He is not kidding.

The Associated Press reported that there will be a deluge of new victims, as many as five thousand more cases that could "surpass anything the nation's clergy sexual abuse crisis has seen before." Lawyers are "fighting for clients with TV ads and billboards asking, 'Were you abused by the Church?'"[13] Dioceses are considering bankruptcy.

---

[13] Bernard Condon and Jim Mustian, "Surge of New Abuse Claims Threatens Church Like Never Before," AP News, December 1, 2019, https://apnews.com/article/621efb9528384f278c71a 97308404531.

The story quotes a seventy-one-year-old woman who claims to have been "raped repeatedly" in a confessional back in the 1950s. Experts believe settlements in such cases will exceed the $350,000 national average per child-sex-abuse case since 2003. California opened a one-year window to new cases in 2003, and the average settlement per victim rose to $1.3 million. Estimated payouts in California, New York, and New Jersey range from $1.8 billion to $6 billion.

New York state opened a one-year window in the summer of 2019, and four hundred cases were filed on the first day alone. The docket has grown to one thousand cases.

Anxious about huge payouts and fearful of how big they can get if cases go to juries, dioceses are setting up slush funds to settle claims with those who agree not to go to court. New York archbishop Timothy Dolan set one up in 2016. To date, it has shelled out more than $67 million to 338 claimants with an average payment of $200,000 each. All five dioceses in New Jersey, three in Colorado, seven in Pennsylvania, and six in California have opened similar funds.

One hopes that such funds can forestall bankruptcy, which has been declared already by twenty dioceses or religious orders. The most recent was the Diocese of Rochester, which listed claims and other debts totaling half a billion dollars.

It is perhaps the devil's greatest trick. Sick homosexual men were allowed to enter the priesthood. They proceeded to harm the bodies and souls of young men and boys. The bishops we were given have been, for whatever reason, incapable of dealing with these horrific crimes. But what is most diabolical is that society at large has made homosexuals into a protected and largely "sympathetic" class so that any efforts by the Church to fix this problem require condemnation of this sympathetic and protected class.

So perhaps now we are at the cold, wet bottom of the abyss, where we find that the nation is consumed by sexual perversion, the number of lost souls is incalculable, and hope is hard to find. But do not be afraid. There is, I promise, a straightforward pathway out. It will be easier to find, however, if we go back to the beginning and see how we lost our way.

2

The Rise of the New State Church

The United States is historically a Christian country, that is, it was founded by Christians and its population remains largely Christian to this day. The speeches and statements of our presidents, our official holidays, the prayers that are said before the opening of Congress and the Supreme Court, the imagery we see on official buildings all attest to the religious, indeed Christian, foundation of our nation. Indeed, the Supreme Court in an 1892 decision declared explicitly that "we are a Christian nation."

Nevertheless, at least until recent days, Americans have understood that we live in a pluralistic society where Protestants, Catholics, Jews, indeed, even atheists, were equal before each other and equal before the law. There was no official church at the federal level that would require belief, assent, or obedience. This is not to say that there have not been dark times in our history when we failed to live up to our ideals. Catholics may recall times when our churches were burned and there were riots against us. But the highest American aspiration has always been that all should be treated equally, that a Jew should get the same treatment in a court of law as a Methodist or a Muslim.

Our twin understanding of our country's deep religious roots coupled with an ideal of religious freedom grew out of the English tradition of religious toleration. The English had an official state church, but the English also recognized the importance of providing dissenters with some measure of freedom. The Act of Toleration of 1689 provided this freedom.

However, the Act distinguished between the rights of individuals to their own private beliefs and the corporate freedom of an institutional church to act in the public square. For example, certain sects could meet privately, but their meetings had to be registered with the state, and they were not allowed public expression. Dissenters from the state church certainly could not hold public office. The Catholic Church, an institution that threatened the established church, was expressly excluded from the Act of Toleration.

This question of whether religious toleration extends merely to individuals, such as a Christian baker, or whether it also attaches to institutions, such as the Catholic Church or even to organizations such as the Boy Scouts or companies such as Hobby Lobby, is one of the most fundamental religious questions in America today. This question was apparent when the Obama administration began shifting terminology from freedom of religion, a broad category that includes public action, to freedom of worship, which is permitted only in places, including churches, that are strictly segregated from the public square.

These thorny issues were of great concern to the American Founders, so much so that they concluded that it was unwise to have an established state church the way the English did; that it would be better to let the various religious groups compete in the public square. So, for example, when the Commonwealth of Virginia considered assessing a tax that would have benefited the teachers of the Christian religion, there were many petitions made against this tax, none more famous than James Madison's

"Memorial and Remonstrance." Madison argued that the tax was a coercive imposition of religion on those who may disagree, and therefore a possible violation not just of conscience but of man's duty to the Creator, which comes prior to his duty to the state. Madison mentions "duty" seven times in the text.

As Madison explicated, where there is an established state church, the punishment of dissenters can easily result. In a letter to William Bradford, young Madison expressed his horror that some religious dissenters to the Anglican faith in Virginia had been jailed. Indeed, Madison enshrined this notion in the First Amendment of the Constitution. He believed that men should not be coerced by the state into accepting a moral code they did not believe in. Keep this in mind as we later explore how a new faith is being imposed upon schoolchildren.

It is important to note that the discussion of freedom of worship, and the openness of the public square, was carried on almost entirely among men who were either practicing Christians or had been raised according to a Christian worldview. Their concern for their neighbors' rights sprang directly from Christ's admonition to love one's neighbor. So, although the government, the law, and the state did not technically dictate a state religion, the society at large—from which the government sprang—maintained it by default. Or, as John Adams famously wrote, "Our Constitution was made only for a moral and religious people. It is wholly inadequate to the government of any other."[14]

Yet, the tension between the religiosity of the people and the purported neutrality of the state to religion has always been

[14] John Adams to Massachusetts Militia, October 11, 1798, Founders Online, https://founders.archives.gov/documents/Adams/99-02-02-3102.

apparent and explains two competing stories about us: one that says we are a Christian nation, that Christianity has pride of place among all faiths, and that the roots of our governmental system are found in the Bible. The other says our government, and by extension the public square, must be secular—that is, strictly neutral with respect to religion and even with respect to God. Each side can show historical warrant for its argument.

The question we must consider is whether it is possible for a government to be completely neutral with respect to the deepest truths.

Professor Steven D. Smith of the University of San Diego School of Law discusses the two views of the nation.[15] He calls one the "providentialist" and the other the "secularist" view. He writes, "Providentialists declare that God works in history, that it is important as a people to acknowledge this providential superintendence, and that the community should actively instill such beliefs in children as a basis for civic virtue." Secularists, on the other hand, "insist that acknowledgments of deity (if there is one) ought to be purely private, and that government acts improperly if it enters into religion or expresses or endorses religious beliefs. Thus, what one constituency views as imperative, the other regards as forbidden."

Many others have recognized these two strains in America's view of itself. In his book *Divided by God*, Noah Feldman of the Harvard Law School describes one as "values evangelicals" and the other as "legal secularists." James Davison Hunter, who wrote

---

[15] Professor Smith discusses this in many of his published books and papers, including *The Rise and Decline of American Religious Freedom* (Harvard University Press, 2015) and *Pagans and Christians in the City: Culture Wars from the Tiber to the Potomac* (Eerdmans, 2018).

the influential book *Culture Wars: The Struggle to Define America*, referred to the two camps as "orthodox" and "progressive." The orthodox camp is defined by "the commitment on the part of adherents to an external, definable, and transcendent authority" that tells us "what is good, what is true, how we should live, and who we are." Hunter argues that the progressives, even the religious ones, place their trust in "personal experience or scientific rationality."[16]

These two views naturally play out in different ways in the political and policy arenas. But importantly, they inform their adherents' understanding of who we are as a nation. Are we a religious nation, or are we a secular nation? The problem is acute because while incompatible beliefs that are purely abstract can be maintained by individuals, the physical world that we live in inevitably requires some specific answers to this question, whether in the expressed public statements of our leaders, the ceremonies we carry out, the words on our money, our national motto—and even, and perhaps especially, in what and how we teach our children.

Since we have tried as a people to avoid making an explicit commitment to one worldview in the form of an established state church, and because disparate views find warrant in our history and in our founding documents, there has been a competition in our society from the beginning as to which viewpoint will dominate. At various times, the providentialists have had the upper hand; and at other times the secularists have dominated. Professor Smith calls this the "principle of open contestation"[17]

---

[16] James Davison Hunter, *Culture Wars: The Struggle to Define America* (New York: Basic Books, 1991), 44.

[17] Steven D. Smith, *The Rise and Decline of American Religious Freedom* (Cambridge, MA: Harvard University Press, 2014), 10.

and explains that the competition has been similar to the competition between the political parties. Sometimes the Democrats win, sometimes the Republicans. But the federal government has tried to avoid explicitly taking a side.

Indeed, to preserve this delicate, and unnatural, balance of a religious people with a religious worldview governed by a secular government with no explicit religious commitment, Thomas Jefferson deployed the idea of a "wall of separation between church and state."[18] This "wall of separation" appears nowhere in our founding documents, but only in a letter from Jefferson to the Danbury Baptist Association. Yet in 1947, it became an explicit precedent of the Supreme Court in the *Everson v. Board* case. The case applied the Establishment clause to forbid the establishment of a state religion by the individual states, rather than simply restricting the clause to the federal government. Ironically, the case upheld certain kinds of public funding for sectarian schools, but explicitly excluded "religion" from part of the public square. As a result, the Court began to disturb the delicate balance that American society had historically maintained. Why? Because secularism itself is as much of a comprehensive worldview as any religion; therefore, at the limit, it is the functional equivalent of a religion, and yet its operation in the public was left unrestricted. What happened in the *Everson* case is that the Supreme Court put a thumb on the scale in what has become known as the Culture War. They did not come down on the side of Christians. They came down on the side of a nascent, but now a fully flowered, established church.

The "wall of separation" is now routinely invoked by Leftists who tell us that we may not bring our faith into the public

18 Jefferson to Danbury Baptists, January 1, 1802, Library of Congress, https://www.loc.gov/loc/lcib/9806/danpre.html.

debate. How often do we hear things like "We cannot consider your objection to abortion because we do not live in a theocracy and your objection is based on your religious faith"? Have you been in an argument over gay marriage? I would bet you didn't even try to make a religious case because you knew it would be shut down immediately. You might even have internalized the notion that your religious beliefs cannot inform public policy. Certainly, if you tried to mention them, your interlocutor would sneer, "We have a wall between church and state in this country." And yet secular beliefs — which are often as much matters of faith as any religious beliefs — are admitted without comment.

As Professor Smith explains, "the Founders did see a place for religion in public policy."[19] Indeed, it is unavoidable. So, the "wall" was never intended to exclude religious arguments from the public square. It was never intended to prevent American citizens from making religious arguments on public policy matters. The "wall" does not even keep the institutional Church out of the debate. Indeed, the U.S. Conference of Catholic Bishops has a capable lobby shop that advances Church beliefs and interests in government deliberations.

Neither does the "wall" keep us personally from serving in government posts; indeed, there is a constitutional prohibition of a religious test for office in the United States. But this has not stopped some senators from hectoring candidates for federal judgeships about their religious beliefs. Remember Senator

---

[19] Quoted in Christopher Shea, "America the Religious?," *Boston Globe*, March 30, 2014, https://www.bostonglobe.com/ideas/2014/03/29/america-religious/qYlT9obGhIY5I3NtE2r7LK/story.html.

Feinstein's ominous questioning of then-Notre Dame law professor Amy Coney Barrett? Remember the judicial candidates asked about their membership in the Knights of Columbus?

But of course, most of us would never cite Scripture or encyclicals in making a public-policy argument. Sometimes it's prudent, but often, sadly, it is because we have internalized the secularist assertion that such arguments are simply not allowed in our discourse. Even worse, if you are a recognizably religious person making secular arguments, using social science, you may still be told "there is a wall of separation between church and state." What has evolved is that religious folks may not make any arguments at all if even their *motivation* is perceived to be religious. Indeed, this very accusation was leveled at lawyers in federal court making arguments in favor of traditional marriage.

The problem is that the "wall" is now perceived in a manner that is diametrically opposed to the way it was originally intended. Jefferson intended the "wall" and indeed the First Amendment itself to be our protectors, to be used as weapons to defend our rights. But now, as I will elaborate upon in due course, whenever the "wall" is breached, it is always by the state as it encroaches upon our religious liberties, both individual liberties and the liberty of the institutional Church.

How did this all happen? After the Supreme Court unbalanced the competition between the providentialists and the secularists, the Court began to promulgate, according to its own sense, the proper role, or lack thereof, of religion in society. In the 1962 school prayer decision, *Engel v. Vitale*, the Supreme Court rushed the field and took the side of the secularists.

On a personal note, when I told my wife that I would be writing critically about the school prayer decisions of the early

sixties, she was surprised. Though she is thoroughly conservative and deeply religious, she is a graduate of an elite law school
and assumed the rightness of the school prayer decisions of the
early 1960s. This is how deeply all of us have imbibed the idea
that these cases were rightly decided. After all, we do not want
Catholic children to be reciting Protestant prayers, do we? And
it also simply seems right that school administrators and school-
teachers should not be leading our children in prayer. That would
be, well, weird—dare I say, even unconstitutional.

But remember, prayer in school was not practiced everywhere
in these United States prior to 1962. In fact, school prayer occurred chiefly in the eastern United States and in the South. It
was relatively rare in the Midwest and in the West. So, managing
school prayer was exactly the sort of local issue that our federal,
decentralized system was designed to handle.

Engel v. Vitale was brought by a group of parents in Nassau
County, New York, who were unhappy with what was known as
the Regents' prayer that was then recited in local schools. The
prayer was the product of serious consideration and reflection
by a group of ministers, priests, and rabbis and was endorsed,
quite remarkably at this remove, by the New York Association of
Secondary School Principals, the New York School Boards Association, and the New York Association of Judges of Children's
Courts. The prayer read, "Almighty God, we acknowledge our
dependence upon Thee, and we beg Thy blessings upon us, our
parents, our teachers, and our country."

The first judge to hear the case, no advocate of school prayer,
nonetheless ruled in favor of its constitutionality. His decision
was appealed and affirmed by two more levels of the New York
court system. As Professor Smith points out, "By the time the
case reached the Supreme Court, 11 of the 13 judges who had

considered the case had concluded in favor of the permissibility of school prayer."[20] The U.S. Supreme Court, however, struck down the Regents' prayer in a 6–1 decision. Smith points out the decision likely would have gone 8–1 but for the fact that Felix Frankfurter had suffered a stroke and Justice Byron White had only recently joined the Court.

What will seem strange to you from this remove of more than fifty years is that the reaction against the Court's decision was immediate, widespread, and intense. From coast to coast, newspapers denounced the decision. This would be unthinkable today. Every governor in the country condemned the decision with the lonely exception of New York's Nelson Rockefeller. Signs began to appear around the country saying, "Impeach Earl Warren," then the chief justice of the Supreme Court. Prayer in school was obviously an unremarkable thing, not just to parents and students but also to those we would consider to be elites. As exotic as school prayer may seem to most of us these days, it was profoundly strange for people in those days to think the Supreme Court would reject as unconstitutional something that had gone on in schools since before the Founding.

The *Engel* case was followed the next year by *Abington School District v. Schempp*, in which the Supreme Court said Bible reading was also unconstitutional. Schempp went further and insisted that "the Constitution demands the governments in this country be 'neutral' in matters of religion, and governments can be neutral

---

[20]   Steven D. Smith, "Constitutional Divide: The Transformative Significance of the School Prayer Decisions," Pepperdine Law Review 38, no. 4 (April 20, 2011): 955, https://digitalcommons.pepperdine.edu/cgi/viewcontent.cgi?article=1032&context=plr.

only if they limit themselves to actions serving 'secular' purposes and having primarily '*secular*' effects."[21]

It is worth pausing to note that secularity has had a confused meaning down through the ages. It began as a religious term meaning "to do with this world" as opposed to the transcendent world of eternity. But it was always understood that even the "secular" world fell under the aegis of God. By contrast, in recent decades, it has come to mean "without religion," "without God." So, when our government insists upon secularity defined this way, it is insisting upon a politics and a law without God, without religion—which means, quite obviously, the government's choosing a side in the modern culture wars. Once again, we see the inherent contradiction between neutrality in matters of religion and the insistence upon secularity in purposes and effects. If the government is to be neutral, then how can it insist upon a secularity that, in modern parlance, means without God and religion?

The Court's pretensions to neutrality and secularity have had reverberations far beyond these Supreme Court cases. As I have pointed out, religiously identified folk who enter into public debates are chastised by secular interlocutors on suspicion of violating the separation of church and state, even when they are not making religious arguments. The assumption is that religious people are motivated by religion. Therefore, anything they say violates neutrality, secularity, and the wall of separation. As outrageous as this is, even many religious folks have internalized this point of view.

[21] Steven D. Smith, "Why School Prayer Matters," *First Things* (May 2020), https://www.firstthings.com/article/2020/05/why-school-prayer-matters.

What's more, religious people tend to muzzle themselves because they know they are not allowed to make religiously based arguments. I saw this happen one week during the homosexual "marriage" debate. Tony Perkins, long-time president of the Family Research Council, was on television on a particular Monday making arguments from Scripture. Only a few days later, he was back on television making arguments from social science, citing studies that show children do best when raised by their married biological mother and father. This became the talking point of social and religious conservatives through the entire marriage debate. There was hardly any talk of tradition because tradition was understood as religiously based and therefore impermissible under the purported neutrality of secularity. See how that works?

And what traditional marriage spokesmen ever talked about the manifest immorality of homosexuality and homosexual behavior? The organizations doling out money to run state efforts to block gay marriage were quite explicit that they would not fund any campaign that commented upon the moral question of homosexuality. The only language now permissible in the public square, according to the Supreme Court and accepted by religious conservatives, is the supposedly neutral language of empiricism, science, and secularity. As I recall, the lawyers who argued this case in California at the Ninth Circuit were chided by the homosexual judge for not making any moral arguments about homosexual "marriage." Of course, had they made such arguments, the judge probably would have dismissed them as inadmissible. In just such a marriage case, the Iowa Supreme Court expressed its suspicion that the secular rationales used by defenders of traditional marriage were really a cloak for religious arguments. As my father used to say, "damned if you do, and damned if you don't." My mom would have responded, "can't win for losing."

Look beyond the law courts. Look to the classrooms. Consider the teaching of evolution, creationism, and intelligent design. The court has ruled that school districts may not teach creationism or intelligent design even though intelligent design is a serious scientific area of study. But it is not allowed because it is viewed as religious and therefore a violation of constitutional tenets. Indeed, even apart from intelligent design, not even well-established scientific evidence against Darwin's view may be taught. According to the secular ideology, the only objection to Darwin is religious, and therefore Darwin wins by default.

Seeing a religious sign in the yard of a church, I sometimes joke: Don't they know about the separation of church and state? Or if a television show has a religious theme: Don't they know about the separation of church and state? And this is not terribly far off the mark because the understanding, most especially among the secularists, is that there is absolutely no place for religion in our society except maybe within the four walls of church on Sunday or in the privacy of our own homes. There is no place for public expressions of religious faith.

This is also why the fight has been so centrally located in public schools. There is something about public education, government-sponsored schooling, that tells us who we are as a people. Prayer in public school was unremarkable from our Founding up to the 1960s precisely because we viewed ourselves not just as a religious people but as a Christian people. The fact that religion generally and Christianity specifically may no longer be mentioned approvingly in the public schools demonstrates the degree to which we may have become an entirely different people. And that is not just historical happenstance. This is the deliberate intent of the secularists who have fought to have Christianity removed from the public square and who want us to be a different people.

It should be obvious, then, that the school prayer and Bible-reading decisions of 1962 and 1963 were about more than religion in public schools. They were about the Supreme Court's choosing a side, a side against Christianity. Indeed, after the Court made its choice, it began furiously delineating the contours of the new official state religion. In the 1965 case *Griswold v. Connecticut*, the Court determined that married couples have the constitutional right to use contraception. The Court based this on a general right to privacy that appears nowhere in the Constitution. Seven years later, the Supreme Court in *Eisenstadt v. Baird* extended the same right to contraception to the unmarried. A year later, *Roe v. Wade* ushered in a right to abortion. Twenty years later, *Planned Parenthood v. Casey* further enshrined abortion into constitutional law. It is here that we see the ethereal "mystery passage" penned by Justice Anthony Kennedy that in America, one has "the right to define one's own concept of existence, of meaning, of the universe, and of the mystery of human life." That is not an interpretation of law; it is simply an expression of Tony Kennedy's personal religious beliefs, which, for now, govern the nation.

The sweet mystery-of-life passage reappeared in 2003 in the *Lawrence v. Texas* decision that made homosexual sodomy a constitutional right. As Justice Scalia wrote in his dissent, it was now nearly impossible to think that "homosexual marriage" would not follow from this decision. And as night follows day, this is precisely what the Supreme Court declared in the *Obergefell* decision of 2015. In June 2020, the Supreme Court decided that gender identity is a protected category under the 1964 Civil Rights Act, which forbids discrimination based on sex. Consequently, it is now official government writ that boys must be allowed to shower with girls in high school sports programs.

Keep in mind, there was no groundswell of public opinion for any of these decisions. One hears these days as a truism that "politics is downstream from culture." This false assertion keeps people out of politics, alas. But these cases did not come from the ground up. They came from the top down. Just as there had been no public call to eliminate school prayer, there was no public call to strike down laws on contraception, to make abortion a constitutional right, and certainly no call to con-stitutionalize sodomy, and or to invent sodomitical marriage. These were decisions that found their warrant only in the elite opinions of lawyers, corporate chiefs, news professionals, and the academy.

So, what we have seen in recent decades is the exclusion of Christian argumentation from the public square, and the enshrinement of a new state religion of secularism—without religion, without God—in the same halls of discourse.

Consider that as late as the 1950s, fornication was illegal in at least thirty-eight states. Adultery was illegal in all but five states. Sodomy was illegal in all the states. Even seduction was considered both a tort and a crime. And contraception was for-bidden in most places. Each of these laws reflected fundamental aspects of traditional Christian teaching. By contrast, the new, sex-centered faith idolizes sexual pleasure and indeed the new State Church—really an established State Church of exactly the kind that our Founders feared—has codified this viewpoint. Walter Russell Mead describes this as "a genuine revolution in civilization."[22] In an important new book about Christianity in Europe, French author Oliver Roy considers whether the new faith of the "desiring subject"—whatever we desire to do we have the right and even the obligation to do—may be a current too strong for Christian civilization to resist. And now we have seen how this cult has been enshrined in our laws, and in our democracy, not through the democratic process but through the least democratic means: imposition by the courts.

[22] Walter Russell Mead, "'Is Europe Christian?' Review: Good Faith Estimate," *Wall Street Journal*, April 9, 2020, https://www.wsj.com/articles/is-europe-christian-review-good-faith-estimate-11586473462.

3

The Unholy Inquisition

With the rise of a new state-imposed orthodoxy, so also has now arisen a new priesthood. This priesthood hands down the dogma and enforces the frontiers of acceptable belief and practice. Members of this new priesthood can be easily identified. They are anyone who wears a robe: judges and justices, academics, and scientists. These are the new priests who have seized control of our society and who now promulgate their dogmas. They also identify and hunt down heretics. If you're wondering, that would be you and me and anyone who is a Christian, anyone who believes what the Church teaches about a host of now controversial, even forbidden, topics.

One of the first claims of this newly established State Church is that its dogmas are nothing more than policies derived from an understanding of science. Indeed, there are many uncontroversial scientific truths. But controversial policies are different from truths, and double-blind, peer-reviewed research papers do not provide support for opinions. They are simply a form of secular encyclical. G. K. Chesterton said it best when he observed that we are seeing "a fight of creeds masquerading as policies." He said, "We have actually contrived to invent a new kind of hypocrite. The old hypocrite, Tartuffe or Pecksniff, was a man whose aims were really worldly and practical, while he pretended that they were religious. The new hypocrite is one whose aims are really religious, while he pretends that they are worldly and practical."[23]

Writer Joseph Bottum examined this shift remarkably well in his 2014 book *An Anxious Age: The Post-Protestant Ethic and the Spirit of America.* He argues that the new Puritans are the same as the old Puritans, simply devoid of their Christian beliefs and now on fire for new scoldings. He says this State Church of Christ without Christ has replaced what used to be mainline Protestantism, only now it is a political agenda. Just like the old Puritans, the new Puritans are on the hunt to identify sinners. And, of course, they see sinners everywhere. They see sinners who do not recycle their refuse. They see sinners who do not recognize somebody's personal pronouns. They see sinners who question apocalyptic environmentalism. Their Puritanism is so refined that they see even sinners who accept apocalyptic environmentalism but who heretically question even small parts of the new environmental faith.

They definitely see sinners and heretics who do not recognize their own racism or the inherent racism of all of our institutional systems. Many people have suggested that we are now going through a new Great Awakening similar to what has happened a few times before in our country's history. They call it a Great Awokening, a bit of fun with the new term "woke," which describes an almost spiritual awareness of the wrongs of Western civilization.

Joseph Bottum went down to the Occupy Wall Street demonstrations in September 2011, a precursor to the riots that set American inner cities ablaze in the spring and summer of 2020. Bottom interviewed many of the demonstrators and found that

---

[23] G. K. Chesterton, *What's Wrong with the World*, chap. 3.

they were imbued with a sort of religious fervor and were hungry for people to know that they were good.

How does this established state faith play out? First, understand that there are a variety of aspects to it that you might even call denominations.

The purported belief in science is one of the most important aspects of the State Church, and scientists are among its highest prelates. Consider the debate years ago over embryonic-stem-cell research. The debate grew so intense and so fevered that in 2004, at the Democratic National Convention, practically every speaker talked about it. They were absolutely convinced that this was the issue that would drive President George Bush from office. I vividly remember being on a religious retreat with the Trappists of the Abbey of Gethsemani in rural Kentucky the evening that George Bush announced how he was going to address the issue. I stood in the front yard of the abbey with my phone pressed against my ear as a friend in Washington held her phone to the television so I could hear Bush's announcement that government scientists would not be allowed to derive new stem-cell lines from newly killed human embryos.

The Democrats produced dozens of experts claiming scientific expertise to argue that Bush's position was a triumph of religion over science and that the only objection to the killing of human embryos was religiously based. But of course, the belief that there is no moral sanction against killing human embryos is simply an alternative religious belief. There is no scientific data that supports that conclusion. Nevertheless, we heard the refrain that we are "anti-science" because to be against the orthodoxy and its priesthood is to be against science.

Many white-robed scientists have argued that the world is in danger because of man-made "climate change." This is another claim by the new priesthood that is questioned by the laity at their peril. Admit that you have doubts about apocalyptic man-made climate change, and you will be told you are anti-science. Your credentials will be examined to see if you have any right to opine in any way on the subject. It would be like someone in the Middle Ages questioning the wisdom of the Church. The laity's role is to accept unquestioningly the nuggets of dogma handed down by white-robed masters. If the scientific priesthood decrees that climate change will kill off the polar bears and that the rise of the seas will flood Manhattan, any skepticism is heresy.

So entrenched among the elite is the new climate-change religion that even the pope has argued for it. His long encyclical *Laudato Si'* is a long *cri de couer* about the risk to our "filthy planet" if we do not stop using fossil fuels. A few years ago, one of my colleagues at C-Fam had the temerity to question a high-ranking Vatican official about a Vatican conference on climate change that excluded scientists who challenged the party line. Even questioning the makeup of the speakers at the conference meant that my colleague was accused of being a part of the Tea Party and in the employ of the oil companies. Bishop Marcelo Sánchez Sorondo, chancellor of the Pontifical Academy of Social Sciences, said that the leftist view of climate change was magisterial, and so, like the Church's view of abortion, believers were required to accept it.

In fact, so absolute has the belief in man-made, catastrophic climate change become that even a little bit of heresy can get someone excommunicated from the State Church. Roger Pielke was a fully credentialed expert from the University in Colorado who fully endorsed climate alarmism. He expressed only a slight disagreement about the claim that climate change had increased storms at sea. Part of the dogma is that increased storm damage along coastlines proves an increase in the number or strength of storms that could only have resulted from global warming. Pielke demurred and said increased storm damage along coastlines had more to do with the radically increased building along coastlines, especially the building of expensive waterfront mansions, and that increased damage from storms came about merely because there was more to damage. He was viciously attacked by other members of the climate priesthood and denounced as a climate denier. So intense and incessant were these denunciations that he eventually left the field all together and became a professor of sports medicine.

Extreme environmentalism even takes on aspects of a death cult, says writer Brendan O'Neill at *Spiked*. He watched a gathering of men and women outside a subway station in London last fall. He said, "They swayed and chanted. They preached about end times. 'What will you do when the world gets hot, what, what?' they intoned, conjuring up images of the hellfire they believe will shortly consume mankind. They sang hymns to their God—science." They actually sang hymn-like songs, "We've got all the science / All that we need / To change the world / Alleluia."[24] (They presumably were unaware that *Alleluia* means "Praise the Lord.") These were congregants of the Extinction Rebellion, and their prayer is that the world goes back to a prior age without electricity.

The environmentalists also have the sacrament of confession. In September 2019, NBC News launched a climate confessions

---

[24] Brendan O'Neill, "The Madness of Extinction Rebellion," *Spiked*, October 7, 2019, https://www.spiked-online.com/2019/10/07/the-madness-of-extinction-rebellion/.

web page intoning, "Even those who care deeply about the planet's future can slip up now and then. Tell us: where do you fall short in preventing climate change? Do you blast the A/C? Throw out half your lunch? Grill a steak every week? Share your anonymous confession with NBC news."[25]

One poor sap wrote, "I still eat red meat. I have been trying to like beans for ten years." Another believer confessed, "I still use plastic bags." Yet another stated, "Using too many ziplock storage bags. Trying to stop." Still others wagged fingers in denunciation: "Amazon delivers one order of multiple items in separate packages instead of one. It means more paper, plastic, and gas." Some boasted: "Used to ride my bike until I almost got killed by a guy in an SUV. Now I drive my 20-year-old Honda Accord everywhere."

Environmentalists have sacred rituals, some of which are enforced by the State Church. Chief among them: recycling. In many municipalities, every household now has a separate bin where they solemnly place cans and bottles and paper products. They have faith that this is something that they are required to do and that it will make the planet a better place, even though there's voluminous data to show that recycling has failed because it is not economically efficient. Recycling plants are closing down all over the country. But it is practically impossible to discard religious rituals that have come to mean so much to so many. Among certain sects, if you tell your friends that you do not recycle, they will treat you like a medieval serf denying the divinity of Christ.

[25] Climate Confessions, NBC News, https://www.nbcnews.com/news/specials/climate-confessions-share-solutions-climate-change-n1054791.

Homosexuality Dogma

Another foundational dogma of the new scientific priesthood is that homosexuals are born homosexual and can never change their homosexuality. The scientific priesthood trots out studies that purport to make this case; that there is a gay gene; that gay brains are different from non-gay brains; that some girl babies are awash in testosterone that has made them transgender boys, and some boy babies are exposed to estrogen that has made them transgender girls. Our white-coated priests will tell you that some people are born into the wrong body and that we must use our scientific expertise to make their bodies match what they think their brains are telling them. To question any of this is to be a heretic — a homophobe or a transphobe.

If you dare to venture an opinion on these sacred notions, you must come with your own set of peer-reviewed studies because this is the only language that the new priesthood and its followers can understand or will accept. But even then, they won't accept your opinion if your papers diverge from the revealed truth. Consider the case of Dr. Paul McHugh, the long-time head of psychiatry at the prestigious Johns Hopkins University in Baltimore. Quite famously, the psychiatric center at Johns Hopkins University was the first place in the United States to perform "sex-change" operations. It was the site of one of the more notorious experiments on a child by a heinous doctor named John Money. The experiment was done on a boy whose penis had been burned off in circumcision. Under Money's direction, his parents tried to raise him as a girl, dresses and all. Dr. Money showed him porn so that he would learn to react as a girl. The horrific story is told in great detail in journalist John Colapinto's *As Nature Made Him*. The boy never acclimated to femininity and later chose to live as nature made him. Sadly, he eventually committed suicide.

Under Siege

When Dr. Paul McHugh took over this clinic at Johns Hopkins, he immediately closed the "sex-change" clinic. Some years later, as discussions about a range of sexual issues become increasingly common, McHugh and noted statistician Lawrence Mayer published a paper examining the scientific claims made about homosexuality, sexual orientation, gender identity, and "transgenderism." These two men were among the most accomplished in their fields. But their paper, which not only examined the scientific claims but criticized and even refuted them, got them branded as heretics. They were given the most vicious treatment. Incredibly, even their impeccable academic and professional credentials were questioned.

One of the particularly devious lines of attack against them was that they published their paper in the *New Atlantis*, a journal that is not peer reviewed. They published there for this very good reason: it would have taken them months, perhaps years, to run the gauntlet of a priesthood-reviewed magazine such as the *New England Journal of Medicine*, with no guarantee that their paper would ever be published. On certain controversial questions, even peer-reviewed journals will not stray from the party line. And like the nihil obstat used by the Church to signal no religious objection to the content, peer review signifies orthodoxy as much as truthfulness. To this day, McHugh is widely condemned for his "heretical" views on sexual orientation and gender identity. Indeed, campaigns have been undertaken to pressure Johns Hopkins University to denounce him, something Johns Hopkins so far has resisted.

The terrible, and ironic, news is that even as science has become more politically and ideologically corrupted, public respect for the scientific priesthood is on the rise. According to

Pew Research, Americans' confidence that scientists work in the public interest is up since 2016.[26]

Statistician William Briggs says, "This surprises because we have been tracking how science is becoming woker and woker, the rate increasing noticeably of late."[27] Briggs points to a story in the *Guardian* newspaper in the United Kingdom reporting the scientific conclusion that testosterone increases women's athletic performance. Of course it would, right? Testosterone is the performance-enhancing drug that helped Lance Armstrong get booted out of cycling and stripped of his seven Tour de France victories. But the *Guardian* is not actually talking about "women." The story is about "trans women," that is, men who think they are women and are therefore allowed to participate in women's sports. Of course they have heightened levels of testosterone. They are male.

Sports are a tricky thing because males naturally have more testosterone than females and, therefore, an undeniable, scientifically verifiable competitive advantage. The question becomes then, what to do with "trans women," that is, hairy men with penises and plenty of testosterone. Your head spins reading the story, but the bottom-line shock is that people take scientists seriously, that the public does not laugh them out of the room but rather increasingly looks up to them. It would be a sin to laugh at a priest of the State Church.

[26] Cary Funk, Meg Hefferon, Brian Kennedy, and Courtney Johnson, "Trust and Mistrust in Americans' Views of Scientific Experts," Pew Research, August 2, 2019, https://www.pewresearch.org/science/2019/08/02/trust-and-mistrust-in-americans-views-of-scientific-experts/.

[27] William Briggs, "Pew Says Trust in Scientists Up. How Depressing," William M. Briggs, October 18, 2019, https://wmbriggs.com/post/28345/.

Closely allied to the scientific priesthood is the priesthood of academics. They, too, wear robes of authority. And they, too, promote a new kind of secularity.

"Hey-hey, ho-ho, Western civ has got to go," they chanted as they marched at Stanford University way back in 1987. Jesse Jackson led that march to protest the university's introductory humanities program known as "Western Culture." Western Civ was required for graduation and included all the things that an educated person should know about the canon of Western civilization. The problem with Western civilization is that it is racist, sexist, and homophobic.

As it turns out, the protestors were pushing on an open door. Shortly thereafter, the program refocused on race, class, and gender—the holy trinity of the State Church—under a program called "Cultures, Ideas, and Values." Out went Western culture, and in came the suffocating multiculturalism.

Writing in the *Chronicle of Higher Education* in the winter of 2019, one writer asked, "Are the humanities over? Are they facing an extinction event?"[28] The writer suggested that we have experienced a double secularization. The first he identified as the toppling of Christianity and the rise of secularism as the dominant idea in society. The second secularization has happened in the humanities where high culture has been undone and "the humanities have become merely a rather eccentric option for a small fraction of the population." He says, "As a society, the value of a canon that carries our cultural or, as they once said, civilizational values can no longer be assumed. These values

[28] Simon During, "Losing Faith in the Humanities," *Chronicle of Higher Education*, December 18, 2019, https://www.chronicle.com/article/losing-faith-in-the-humanities/.

are being displaced and critiqued by other ostensibly more enlightened ways of thinking."[29] But this makes sense. A society's culture is a reflection of its "cult," that is, the core religious idea that animates it. If the underlying faith of a society is changed, its culture will necessarily change too.

If you enter into any kind of debate about our once-shared historical knowledge of values, you will inevitably be called a colonizer and a racist. You will be told that Christopher Columbus brought disease and death to a Sylvan Glade of happiness and order. This is why his statues must be torn down.

Social Justice

The goal of genuine social justice is certainly compatible with Christianity. Indeed, Christianity has done more for social justice than anything else in human history. But the politicized poison that masquerades as social justice has caused incalculable damage as it has seeped into official governmental policy.

In the summer of 2020, the federal government began teaching its employees about the evils of what it calls "whiteness." The United States Army has an entire agency dedicated to equity and inclusion. One of its courses, entitled "Operation Inclusion," tells service members that if they support the enforcement of immigration laws or say that "all lives matter," they are white supremacists. No kidding. The course claims that President Trump's campaign slogan "Make America Great Again" was evidence of "covert white supremacy."[30]

---

[29] Ibid.

[30] Hans A. von Spakovsky and Charles "Cully" Stimson, "Teaching Hate Under the Guise of 'Inclusion'—In the U.S. Army,"

It is not just the army. In June 2020, as cities across the nation were burning because of a twisted sense of social justice, a private diversity consulting firm conducted training called "Difficult Conversations about Race in Troubling Times" for federal agencies. The federal agencies included the Treasury Department, the Federal Reserve, the Federal Deposit Insurance Corporation, the Consumer Financial Protection Bureau, the National Credit Union Administration, and the Office of the Comptroller. The training called upon all of these agencies to pledge "allyship amid the George Floyd tragedy." According to whistleblower documents, the training asserts that "virtually all white people contribute to racism." White managers were called upon to create safe spaces where blacks could talk about what it means to be black while white staffers were told to keep silent and "sit in the discomfort" of their racism.[31]

Howard Ross, the man who created the training program, has billed the federal government $5 million since 2006 for such training programs. Even NASA forked over $500,000 for "power and privilege sexual orientation workshops."[32]

These official programs of the federal government can best be understood as a modern form of catechesis for the State Church. That these programs expanded, some say metastasized, even under the Trump administration shows the strength and power of the State Church.

Heritage Foundation, July 21, 2020, https://www.heritage.org/defense/commentary/teaching-hate-under-the-guise-inclusion-the-us-army.

[31] Christopher F. Rufo, "'White Fragility' Comes to Washington," *City Journal*, July 18, 2020, https://www.city-journal.org/white-fragility-comes-to-washington.

[32] Ibid.

None of this started at the federal government. All of it happened first on college campuses under the tutelage of radical professors who came of age as students the 1960s. But, writing about his time at Stanford in the 1960s, Robert Curry says even in those radical times, students would never have thought of trying to eliminate seminal courses. And the professors, many of whom were battle-hardened veterans who had fought for Western civilization in the Second World War, would never have thought about removing it from university curriculums. The students from the 1960s, however, became the professors of the 1980s. That is when Jesse Jackson and his radical crew fulminated for an end to courses on Western civilization, a call that has now transmogrified into an effort to destroy Western civilization itself.

Social Isolation and Excommunication

One of the primary tools of the Left on college campuses and elsewhere is excommunication through political correctness, social isolation, and cancel culture. Human beings have a natural terror of being isolated and alone. The new priesthood and its laity use this to great effect.

Consider my own experience during the COVID panic. For many weeks, even months, I refused to wear a mask, even in the grocery store. This was fine because there were always a few other brave souls and together we presented a kind of united front. Toward the end of summer, I was still unmasked in the grocery store until one day I realized I was the only one. I remained the only one for a while, but then it got to me. It was remarkably uncomfortable being the only one. So I gave in. I masked up. Whether or not masks are efficacious in limiting the spread of disease is not the point. The point is, it is hard to be alone.

Stella Morabito used to work on Soviet propaganda at the Central Intelligence Agency. In recent years, she has shifted her focus to studying how fear is used by the State Church at all levels of society. Morabito has explained how fear of isolation, ironically, drives us further into isolation since we are afraid to express our real views, even to our closest friends, because we fear rejection. In fact, isolation even from your children can occur, since you may be afraid of what they might unknowingly repeat. These fears were especially pronounced under the totalitarian governments that tormented the Soviet Union and Nazi Germany. But they are present in America today as well.

Political correctness and fear of isolation work to enforce the whole spectrum of State Church dogma, particularly with respect to homosexuality, "transgenderism," and climate change.

Here is how it works. Public opinion is first molded through psychological manipulation using techniques such as "saturation" and "suppression," also known as "desensitization" and "jamming." How many times have you heard the phrase "love is love" in relation to the gay movement? I would surmise hundreds of times. You see it in social media. You see it "hashtagged" in the advertisements of major corporations, especially during the now-hijacked month of June. The slogan seems like a truism. It is meant to suggest the idea that people cannot be punished for loving those "whom they happen to love." But its essential meaninglessness is revealed when you consider that it could easily be applied to incest. After all, if "love is love," then what about that kind of "love"? The incessant drumbeat of "love is love" is designed to "saturate" your thoughts, so that you do not think critically. If you hear it enough from important sources, you come to accept it.

And what are these important sources? As Morabito points out, they first included the arts and the academy, followed by Hollywood and the media. After that, "softer targets were absorbed or bought off—legislative bodies, the justice system, corporate America, religion lite."[33] But then she says something shocking. Even the harder targets such as the military, K–12 education, and the more traditional churches can be overcome. Since Morabito wrote this in the fall of 2016, we have seen this ideology rapidly accepted at the highest levels of the military; children as young as five years old are being indoctrinated into gender ideology; many churches are celebrating homosexuality.

The flip side of "saturation" is "suppression," or the silencing of dissenting views. This is where political correctness comes in. More than a decade ago, a man I know, formerly a top executive at Time Inc., was asked by a young man from human resources if he could paste a rainbow decal on his office door. The man declined. You can no longer decline. My friend now has an important job in Silicon Valley. I am quite sure he no longer declines, and it is quite possible that his mind has been saturated, that he now fully supports the LGBT agenda, and that in his own way he now suppresses others.

Consider the case of "transgenderism." There is nothing quite as preposterous as the idea that a man can become a woman just by declaring it. But we now see parents holding gender reveal parties for their teenage children who have concluded they are not actually the sex that they are. In New York City, a small business can be fined up to $250,000 for persistently using the incorrect pronoun to refer to a customer who expresses an alternative

[33] Stella Morabito, "A Creature of Political Correctness," *Human Life Review* (Fall 2016): 60.

personal preference. A burly man wearing a dress comes into your store, and you refuse to refer to him as "her"? You could lose your business. That is suppression.

The purpose of all this is to instill fear. Because of the work that I do at the United Nations and here in the United States, I have lost many old and dear friends whose minds have been saturated. A few years ago, I reached out to someone who had been one of my closest friends in college. It took me a while to get him to respond to my e-mails and eventual phone call. Finally, I succeeded in getting through to him. He told me, "Do not ever try to contact me again." This was a fellow who advised me in college never to let politics become personal.

There are people I have worked with in business over the years, in the magazine publishing world of New York, who won't have anything to do with me now. These are people I worked closely with for years. But I used to be a quiet conservative, worried about rejection.

I remember years ago in New York working up the courage to tell a girlfriend that I was conservative. She arched her eyebrow and asked, "How conservative are you?" Still wary of revealing my true self, I disclosed, "I don't believe in funding for the arts." She laughed out loud. Would she laugh now about LGBT or climate change or the many other deadly serious dogmas of the day? I doubt it. My own sister now tells people that I run a hate group.

The poor kids on college campuses are terrified of stepping outside the very narrow range of acceptable opinion. They are terrified of being exposed and socially burned as heretics. In 2019, researchers studied free expression at the University of North Carolina at Chapel Hill. They asked students "how many times during the semester they kept a sincere opinion related to class to themselves because they were worried about the consequences of expressing it." Surprisingly, they found that even 23 percent of self-identified liberals self-censored; 68 percent of self-identified conservatives self-censored.[34] The only surprise is that the number is so low. Perhaps they were self-censoring even when answering the question.

The researchers also found that the students are more fearful of each other and of the risk of social isolation than they are of getting a bad grade from their almost-universally leftist professors. Consider the case of Kaitlin Bennett, who became famous around the time of her graduation from Kent State University in 2018. She posted a college graduation picture of herself holding an AR-10 rifle. She was widely vilified by leftist students on social media, though she became a hero to students who supported the Second Amendment. Now known as Gun Girl, she started a very popular website called Liberty Hangout. In February 2020, she and a video crew appeared on the campus at Ohio University with the intention of quizzing students on presidential trivia. She wanted to show how uninformed many college students are today. She was able to ask only a single question before a mob of hostile students surrounded her and her crew. That is how famous Gun Girl had become. The crowd grew to several hundred. The campus police refused to protect her, and she escaped to a getaway vehicle only because she had brought her own private security with her. This happened at a large Midwestern state school where you might have expected at least some of the students would be on her side. But as it

---

[34] Timothy Ryan, "What Liberals and Conservatives Get Wrong about Free Expression on College Campuses," *HD Reporter*, February 19, 2020, http://hdreporter.com/education/7299-what-liberals-and-conservatives-get-wrong-about-free-expression-on-college-campuses.

turned out, with very few exceptions, everyone was against her, vociferously and dangerously.

To any conservative student present that day, or any student who watches the video of the incident, the message is abundantly clear: venture from a narrow range of acceptable opinions at your own peril.

Writing at the *American Scholar*, William Deresiewicz says modern liberal arts schools have become religious schools. He writes, "The religion in question is not Methodism or Catholicism but an extreme version of the belief system of the liberal elite: the liberal professional, managerial, and creative classes, which provide a large majority of students enrolled at such places and even larger majority of faculty and administrators who work at them. To attend those institutions is to be socialized, and not infrequently, indoctrinated into that religion."[35]

Today's campus radicals are no longer countercultural. Unlike during the 1960s, the radicalism of today's students is fully supported by the faculty and certainly by the administrations, which don't just cave to student demands but enthusiastically endorse their agenda.

The most disturbing news with respect to social isolation is that it is, in fact, a perfectly rational fear. Social media is routinely scoured for heresy so that dissenters can be punished. Twenty-five-year-old Iowan Carson King held up a sign at a football game asking for Venmo contributions to buy beer. He raised a whopping one million dollars, which he promptly turned over to charity. Then, an ace reporter from the *Des Moines Register*

---

[35] William Deresiewicz, "On Political Correctness," *American Scholar*, March 6, 2017, https://theamericanscholar.org/on-political-correctness/.

inspected Carson's social media history and found unacceptable comments. A frenzy of hate was visited upon Carson, and the charity gave the money back. They cared more for political correctness than the children they serve. Let's hope that, when they gave it back, the kid kept the money!

If there is any good news, it is that the new orthodox are typically unable to defend their positions effectively; heretics are rarely allowed to speak, so the new orthodox are rarely required to defend their positions. There's an old saying in the Catholic Church that heresy is the strength of the Church, because combating heresy tends to sharpen orthodox argument. One of the reasons the new orthodox become so frustrated and resort so quickly to mockery and name-calling is that they cannot justify their own faith.

The new faith has infected all the power centers in our country. Scholar Michael Lind talks about what he calls the managerial elite that "consists of the functionaries of corporations, large investment banks, law firms, government agencies, both civilian and military, nonprofits, and universities." He goes on to say, "they may have professional degrees, but they are essentially organization men and organization women in centralized, hierarchical, bureaucratic entities."[36] Just like students at colleges and universities around the country, the people who work in these entities understand the same narrow range of acceptable opinions. They also fully understand not just the risk of social isolation that comes from expressing heretical views but the professional risk of voicing dissenting opinions.

[36] Michael Lind, "The Double Horseshoe Theory of Class Politics," *Bellows*, July 16, 2020, https://www.thebellows.org/the -double-horseshoe-theory/.

Under Siege

A few years ago, when I was writing for Breitbart, Professor Robert George of Princeton alerted me to worried, indeed frightened, employees at JP Morgan Chase, the fourth-largest financial institution in the world. JPMorgan Chase had initiated a global survey of all their employees. Included in the survey was the question "Are you LGBT, or an ally?" Note there are only two answers to this question; both of them signal your support for an ideology that most Christians consider antithetical to both the common good and to common morality. Christian employees were frightened that, even if they skipped the question, it would be noticed and they would suffer consequences ranging from required participation in a reeducation program, to being overlooked for promotion, to being demoted — or fired.

In my research for the story, I discovered that JPMorgan Chase was one of the largest corporate entities pushing the LGBT agenda. JPMorgan Chase was among the first in the country to festoon their branch banks with rainbow symbols in the month of June, which the Left now celebrates as "Pride Month." But it is not surprising: their corporate website boasts, astonishingly, that more than 10 percent of their top executives identified as LGBT.

Years ago, the sexual Left began infiltrating the human-resources departments of major corporations, as well as their philanthropic arms, which donate hundreds of millions of dollars to left-wing causes. Look at the corporate power achieved by the anti-Christian Human Rights Campaign, a major campaigner for "gay rights."

Early in 2020, the Human Rights Campaign (HRC) released its annual Corporate Equality Index, a measurement of how major corporations are adhering to the demands of the homosexual Left. The Corporate Equality Index lists 1,059 corporations and how they go about favoring all things LGBT. The report's executive summary explains, "Where businesses enumerate federally protected categories of workers in their non-discrimination policies (e.g., based on race, religion, disability, etc.), the HRC Foundation evaluates them on the inclusion of 'sexual orientation' and 'gender identity' protections."

It should be noted that this report was released at Davos, the annual gathering of some of the world's most powerful people. This certainly gives the lie to the notion that homosexuals are marginalized and powerless. The message is clear: corporations must step in line with the homosexual elite not only with policy changes but also with cold, hard cash, millions of dollars of it.

For example, the HRC report measures not only the provision of health insurance for same-sex couples but even the availability of "sex-change" coverage and other forms of transgender promotion. Indeed, the report measures businesses' advocacy for LGBTs in "advertising, public policy engagement, supplier diversity, philanthropy, and sponsorship."

When Big Gay winks, corporate America smiles. More than 1,000 corporations have voluntarily participated in the HRC questionnaire, including almost all of the Fortune 500. Fully 91 percent of the Fortune 500 companies have gender-identity protection enumerated in their nondiscrimination policies, and 98 percent of those businesses offer such protections. Eighty-nine percent of reporting businesses offer "sex-change" coverage. Indeed, 686 of the companies reporting, or 64 percent of the total, have achieved a score of 100 percent.

Corporations that have not instituted the desired policies become targets for outside pressure groups, shareholders, suppliers—and even the Jezebel wives of henpecked board members. When former secretary of state Rex Tillerson headed ExxonMobil, the largest oil company in the world, his company received a zero score from HRC. Its score is now 85 percent. After all, there's nothing quite so gay as the oil business.

U.S. Steel wised up, too. Its score went from 20 percent in 2019 to 100 percent in the 2020 report. The score of the law firm Holland & Hart, one of the largest in the world, went from 35 percent to 100 percent in a single year. In fact, almost all of the major law firms in the country now have ratings of 100 percent. Is it any wonder that it is nearly impossible for those supporting traditional marriage and traditional notions of human sexuality to find high-quality legal representation in court? Law firms are afraid of those kinds of clients.

The list of corporations bullied by the HRC hustle goes on and on. The toy company Mattel went from 65 percent to 100 percent in one year. So did Sony Interactive Entertainment. Discovery Communications, owner of the Discovery Channel, the Learning Channel, and much else, languishes at 20 percent because they don't pay for "sex changes." No doubt this will be rectified soon.

What happens when all of corporate America gets a 100 percent score on the HRC's Equality Index? Will Big Gay organizers go quietly back to their lives? Unlikely. Power is attractive, and there's always more to do, more pockets to pick, more heretics to harass. The HRC owns a spectacular building in downtown Washington, D.C., only a few blocks from the White House. They bring in fifty million dollars a year. This gay cash does not grow on trees. It is shaken out of scared individuals and major corporations who originally paid protection money for peace but now are genuinely committed to the gay agenda. When the homosexuals came knocking, they found they were pushing on an open door.

But it is not homosexuality alone that has seduced corporate boards. The entire gamut of racial and sexual issues is now a motivating force for many major institutions. For example, in January 2020, Goldman Sachs's CEO David Solomon announced (from Davos) that his company, Wall Street's biggest underwriter of initial public offerings, would no longer take public any companies that did not have a director who is either female or "diverse." Goldman Sachs will also decline "financial assistance" to nascent companies whose directors are all "straight, white, men."[37] BlackRock, Inc. and State Street Global Advisors quickly followed suit. The NASDAQ recently announced that all companies listed on its exchange had to have a "diverse" board. Out with straight white males, in with the rainbow. As a management professor at Boston University said, "It's what big investors are looking for these days. If the board has all white males, that is a big negative."[38]

But there is more than the private markets at work here. Governments are getting into the act as well. A company with an all-male board now can be fined $100,000 by the State of California. This is the new State Church in action.

Once the Supreme Court handed down its diktat on same-sex "marriage," efforts to squelch heretical dissent have increased. It is increasingly difficult to publish in any newspaper, large or small, anything critical of homosexuality in general or homosexual "marriage" in particular. A few years ago, I was commissioned to

---

[37] Elisa Martinuzzi, "Goldman's Anti-Bro Pledge Isn't Just a Stunt," *Bloomberg*, January 24, 2020, https://www.bloomberg.com/ opinion/articles/2020-01-24/goldman-sachs-is-right-to-reject -the-all-white-all-male-board.

[38] Jeff Green, "Goldman to Refuse IPOs If All Directors Are White, Straight Men," *Bloomberg*, January 23, 2020, https:// www.bloomberg.com/news/articles/2020-01-24/goldman-rule -adds-to-death-knell-of-the-all-white-male-board.

write a column for the *New York Post* about a law being debated in the New York City Council that would have banned talk therapy for anyone of any age who sought help with unwanted same-sex thoughts, desires, or behaviors. The *New York Post* editors insisted that I say that such talk therapy *should* be banned for people under the age of eighteen. I declined, and the piece never ran.

When the *Obergefell* decision was imposed, a news outlet in Pennsylvania—PennLive/*Patriot-News*—announced that it would "very strictly limit op-eds and letters to the editor in opposition to same-sex marriage. These unions are now the law of the land. And we will not publish such letters and op-eds any more than we would publish those that are racist, sexist, or anti-Semitic."[39] There you have it. The Christian—indeed, the nearly universal, global, commonsense understanding—that marriage unites one man and one woman is now considered by the editors of this outlet to be the equivalent of racism, sexism, or anti-Semitism.

This is how the State Church works. A doctrinal decision is made by the high priesthood, and the major power centers fall into line. Brendan Eich, the inventor of Mozilla, lost his own company when it was revealed that he had contributed a small amount to the traditional-marriage campaign in California. His donation was discovered in IRS documents illegally leaked by a government employee. Now, a movement has begun to compel nongovernment organizations to disclose the names and addresses of all of their donors. The chilling effect this would have on freedom of expression is obvious.

---

[39] PennLive Editorial Board, "The Supremes Got It Right—It's No Longer 'Gay Marriage.' It's 'Marriage.' And We're Better for It: Editorial," PennLive/*Patriot-News*, updated January 5, 2019, https://www.pennlive.com/opinion/2015/06/gay_marriage_anthony_kennedy_o.html.

The state of Florida has a large, sophisticated school voucher program to which corporations can contribute money to help pay the tuition of students seeking to leave public schools and attend private and religious schools. This Florida program helped more than twenty thousand students escape public schools and receive a better education. But the *Orlando Sentinel* discovered that at least 156 private schools that take state scholarships espouse anti-gay views. Donors to the program immediately fell in line. ABC Fine Wine and Spirits said, "ABC would never knowingly donate to any organization that discriminates and we strongly encourage an immediate review by the Florida Department of Education into the policies of the scholarship fund."[40] A major Florida hotelier abruptly ended his support for the program. Major banks such as Wells Fargo and Fifth Third halted their contributions to the scholarship fund.

The *Orlando Sentinel* examined documents from more than 1,000 private religious schools and found that 156 had policies which, on religious grounds, disagreed with Leftist views of sexual orientation and gender identity. One school, Mount Dora Christian Academy, said, "professing immorality (including homosexuality) is a "level III offense,"[41] an infraction that would be punishable by suspension and possible expulsion. There are more than 2,000 schools in the program. Yet the entire program was written off by corporate donors because 15 percent of the schools held traditional views of sexual morality.

---

[40] Annie Martin and Leslie Postal, "Gay-Friendly Companies Financially Support Anti-LGBTQ Florida Private Schools," *Orlando Sentinel*, January 23, 2020, http://www.orlandosentinel.com/news/education/os-ne-business-donations-tax-credit-20200123-xdzohcbw7zgfhnrmgtfniykn6u-htmlstory.html.

[41] Ibid.

So much for toleration and diversity of viewpoint in the State Church.

Consider what happened to the state of Indiana when the state legislature passed a religious-freedom bill that would have protected small businesses from having to participate in activities that violate their religious freedom. The sexual Left perceived the threat to their agenda. Corporate strongmen, such as homosexual Apple CEO Tim Cook, condemned the new law. So did the NCAA. Salesforce threatened to pull its business out of the state. Republican governor Mike Pence caved within forty-eight hours and vetoed the bill.

When the state of North Carolina made it illegal for men and boys posing as women to use restrooms and showers of the opposite sex, the National Basketball Association indicated that it might pull the 2017 All-Star game then scheduled to take place in North Carolina's largest city, Charlotte. Arizona's Governor Jan Brewer vetoed a religious-freedom bill after the National Football League threatened to pull the Super Bowl from the state. In the late spring of 2019, the AMC television network threatened to relocate filming of the hit show *The Walking Dead* out of Georgia if the state passed a restrictive abortion bill.

Although, in some instances, corporate pressure has been deployed against recalcitrant states, at the federal level, government-imposed orthodoxy is permeating more and more of the bureaucracy. A few years ago, I presented the chapter on "transgenderism" from my book *Fake Science* to a Rotary Club in the tony Washington, D.C., suburb of Great Falls. During the question-and-answer period, a man challenged my view on "transgenderism" saying, "We in the military will incorporate transgender soldiers with the same ease we incorporated gay soldiers." The man is an air force general.

It is a rare to encounter a high-ranking military officer who is not weak and political. Most have their eyes trained primarily on their next promotion. So it should not surprise us much that military officers, particularly of the higher ranks, enthusiastically endorse the latest fashions. Couple this ideological weakness with civilian control of the military, and you discover that the military turns out not to be one of the hardest targets for State Church ideologues to conquer, but rather one of the softest targets.

Almost immediately after the military's "don't ask, don't tell" policy was eliminated and actively homosexual men and women began to serve in the armed forces, military leaders began to persecute Christians, with special attention paid to military chaplains. In 2015, naval chaplain Wes Modder says he was relegated by his superiors to doing nothing more than sitting alone in the base chapel, forbidden from speaking to sailors who may have needed Christian counseling. Why? Because Modder had fallen prey to a secret and private investigation by a homosexual sailor who was volunteering in Modder's office. As I reported on Breitbart in the spring of 2015, this junior officer, who had identified himself as a devout Catholic, had attended Modder's briefings, as well as his classes on marriage, and would often wander in for private conversations with Modder. They talked about a lot of issues but never about homosexuality. It never came up. What's more, the spy never identified himself as homosexual. Even so, this junior officer charged the chaplain with making homophobic slurs, which Modder denied. The simple fact was that Modder, as a chaplain in the military, had simply preached the Christian faith.

Modder's superior relieved him of his duties, removed him from the promotions list, and initiated procedures to have him removed *involuntarily* from the military. In a sharply worded memo, his commanding officer said Modder was a threat to unit cohesion. Note, this was the charge that traditionally kept gays out of the military. Now it is being used by the new orthodox either to keep Christians quiet or to have them expelled. Modder was specifically charged with failure to show "tolerance and respect" to gays and failing to "function in the diverse and pluralistic environment" of the base — though, ironically, it is the State Church that appears incapable of being "pluralistic."

Modder's attorneys asked the navy to allow Modder the "religious accommodation" that is allowed by law. The request was denied. Consider this closely: a Christian chaplain was forced to apply for a religious accommodation so that he could teach his faith, which is shared by a large percentage of soldiers. The government said no.

At the time, Modder had served his country for almost twenty years, including in several war zones. But none of this proved sufficient to defend against sanction by the government-backed religious orthodoxy.

All of this happened at roughly the same time that the U.S. Army approved hormone therapy for male soldiers who want to be women. Secretary of Defense Ash Carter had declared that "gender dysphoria" would no longer be sufficient cause to disqualify anyone from military service. Subsequently, the armed services announced that taxpayers would begin paying for full-blown "sex-change" operations. So strong is this new religious fervor in the military that post-op transsexuals are allowed to serve even when they are not allowed to deploy to a war zone. Why can't they deploy? Because all of them need a lifetime supply of hormones, and the hormones require refrigeration, which is not readily available in most war zones. Normally, soldiers who cannot deploy for six straight months are discharged. Does anyone suppose the acolytes of the new orthodoxy will suffer this fate?

President Trump ended the practice of allowing transsexuals into the military. But the state religion is now so well established in the bureaucracy that it is certain that they will return. Consider the fate of a woman service member taking a shower confronted by a naked man who says he is a woman. Will she be subject to charges if she averts her gaze or covers up? Will that create a hostile atmosphere incompatible with unit cohesion?

The military is attacking not simply individual clerics but entire ministries. In 2015, U.S. Army active duty and reserve troops at Camp Shelby were told that the American Family Association is a domestic hate group because of the positions it takes on the family and homosexuality. A chaplain who was present at the briefing interrupted and said that the American Family Association could not be considered a domestic hate group. But the briefer asserted, "AFA could be considered a hate group because they don't like gays." The soldiers present were informed that they could face punishment for participating in organizations that are considered hate groups. Yet another briefing told officers to watch for troops who supported groups such as the socially conservative Family Research Council. One officer said the two Christian groups did not "share our army values." Focus on the fact that these were actions of *government* officials; rather than acting in a neutral way, they are actively enforcing a new and perverse orthodoxy.

In 2015, the Family Research Council issued a lengthy report on discrimination against Christians in the military. It noted that in 2011, the Houston National Cemetery was sued for preventing Christian prayers from being said at military funerals. Also in 2011, an ethics training course for nuclear missile officers at Vandenberg Air Force Base was suspended because it used Christian reading materials. In 2012, the archbishop of the Archdiocese of Military Services issued a letter to Catholic chaplains urging service members to resist implementation of the Health and Human Services contraceptive mandate in Obamacare. The letter was censored by the Obama administration. In 2013, a U.S. Air Force officer was told he could not have a Bible on his desk because it might appear that he was condoning a particular religion. The examples abound of Christianity and Christians being trampled by the new orthodoxy in a military setting.

The situation is equally dire at the local level. Atlanta fire chief Kelvin Cochran published a book privately that expressed the traditional Christian view that homosexuality is immoral. His book was intended to help men overcome guilt from past sins, such as "whatever is opposite of purity; including sodomy, homosexuality, lesbianism, pederasty, bestiality, all other forms of sexual perversion." As a result, he was suspended without pay for a month pending an investigation into whether his thoughts violated city policy or discriminated against city employees. A subsequent report demonstrated that his personal religious beliefs had no impact on how he treated employees under him. Nevertheless, he was fired.

Eric Moutsos served as a policeman with the Salt Lake City Police Department until he was hounded out of his job for his views. Moutsos is a Mormon with the normal, traditional beliefs about human sexuality. His infraction centered on a gay-pride parade where he was asked to do motorcycle choreography. He told his superiors he did not want to be an active participant in the parade, but that he would be willing to provide traffic control and public safety services. Moutsos reports, "The police department suspended me, took away my gun and badge, and told me that I would be investigated for discrimination."[42] The department misrepresented his views to the news media, saying he refused even to work security and traffic assignment, and he was immediately branded a bigot. As I reported at Breitbart, Moutsos had been praised a few years before for his sensitive handling of two men "protest-kissing" at a Mormon church. As he stated, "In my duties as a police officer, I have been called upon to protect events I disagree with, including several LGBT rallies."[43] But the State Church cannot countenance any kind of heresy.

Some may say that we have not gone as far as to establish a new State Church. But nuanced disputes about terminology do not alter the fact that these men in the military, the fire department, and the police department were dismissed from their jobs because of their Christian beliefs, according to laws duly passed and enforced by the highest levels of our government. Those are the actions of an established state church, call it whatever you will.

Education

As I have already discussed, government schools are instrumental in defining who we are as a people. Policymakers, politicians, educators, and ideological busybodies all understand that schools do far more than simply teach reading, writing, and arithmetic. They inculcate our national identity. Schools proclaim who

---

[42] Austin Ruse, "Policeman Claiming He Was Forced Out over LGBT Controversy Mulls Lawsuit," Breitbart, February 27, 2015, https://www.breitbart.com/politics/2015/02/27/policeman-claiming-he-was-forced-out-over-lgbt-controversy-mulls-lawsuit/.

[43] Ibid.

we are as a people. For decades, it was uncontroversial that we were, in important ways, a Christian people. Though the federal government was not formed as a Christian religious body, it was nevertheless widely recognized that we were a Christian people prior to our Founding, during our Founding, and long after our Founding. Indeed, despite the new legal sanctions that have established an alternate, religious viewpoint within our government, we are still demographically a Christian people to a large degree. But elites in government and in the private sector have converted to a new faith, and to promote it, they have refashioned our laws accordingly. Is it any surprise that this new religion is now being taught in our schools?

Consider that five- and six-year-old children are now being taught that sex is not physically determined at conception but is subjectively decided upon by a doctor in a delivery room. They are taught that delivery-room sex assignment can be wrong, unfair, and even a violation of human rights. They are told that each of us has the right to determine our own gender. None of this is based even remotely on empirical evidence about the material world. It is not based in science; science has found no transgender gene, just as science has not found the elusive gay gene.

What they are teaching small children are ideas based on faith alone. They are teaching the tenets of a new religion. The new priests of the new religion have gotten as powerful as the priests of Baal once were. But make no mistake about it: there is nothing secular or neutral about this new State Church. It is partisan, and it is vicious.

Writing in the religious journal *First Things*, social critic Mary Eberstadt points out that this new church of the sexual revolution has a primary target, and that is the Christian faith, specifically church teachings with regard to sexual morality. She says correctly that the new faith of secularism is a competitor to be vanquished. In June 2016, when the Supreme Court struck down the Texas law requiring abortion clinics to meet the standards of surgical clinics, abortion advocates celebrated on the steps of the Court. Eberstadt described them as "gyrating, weeping, waving, screaming … women behaving as if they were in the throes of religious ecstasy."[44]

Eberstadt further drives the point home in describing the women's march on Washington after the election of Donald Trump. She writes, "This public demonstration, too, was driven in large degree by a single force: animus against traditional Judeo-Christian moral teaching—specifically, teaching about sex."[45] She recalled the totemic hats the women wore that day, replicas of female genitalia.

Scott Alexander, writing at his influential blog *Slate Star Codex*, tells the story of attending an Easter parade in Guatemala. It was a garish, all-night, cacophonous celebration of not merely religious faith but a community's identity as a people. Easter parades, with up to a million people, used to happen in New York. Judy Garland and Fred Astaire starred in a famous movie called *Easter Parade* in 1948. These parades have now been taken over by flamboyant homosexuals and their fellow travelers. The same city officials, congressmen, business leaders, Boy Scouts, local high school marching bands, representatives of the local car dealership, and members of many of the local churches who once marched in Easter parades now march to proclaim this new faith.

---

[44] Mary Eberstadt, "The Zealous Faith of Secularism," *First Things* (January 2018), https://www.firstthings.com/article/2018/01/the-zealous-faith-of-secularism.

[45] Ibid.

Under Siege

How did we get here? How did we arrive at a place where a novel religion has supplanted Christianity at the highest levels of our state? We've seen how the Supreme Court breached the wall of church and state, and how it has abused the Establishment Clause. But there are, I think, even deeper forces at work that are far older, and far more powerful, than the law. Our country is now in the grip of the old and vicious false gods that have tormented humanity from the very beginning. In the end, ours is a spiritual crisis.

4

Old and Vicious Gods Are Come Again

Alexis de Tocqueville saw some of this coming. In an often-overlooked passage of *Democracy in America*, Tocqueville made the rather astounding claim that Americans would eventually have to decide between pantheism and Catholicism. Consider that he wrote this in the 1840s, at a time when various strains of Protestantism held a grip on the United States, and Catholicism in many places was barely tolerated. There's a strong argument to be made that this is roughly the choice that is before us now, here in the second decade of the twenty-first century: pantheism or Catholicism, paganism or Catholicism, some kind of new ism and Catholicism. But a look at Tocqueville and his argument is helpful.

Writing at the Law and Religion Forum, Robert Delahunty explained that Tocqueville believed that Calvinism would devolve into a form of natural religion similar to what he saw in Unitarianism. This transformation would occur chiefly among American elites; regular folks would be drawn to Catholicism. And indeed, the collapse of mainline Protestantism and the elite's enthusiastic embrace of pagan sexual practices support Tocqueville's prediction, as does the continuing stream of conversions by Evangelical leaders to the Catholic Church.

Joseph Bottum develops this theme extensively in his wonderful book *Anxious Age*. What he describes as happening within the collapsing mainline denominations is a declining attention to the sweet by-and-by and an increasing interest in the here and now. But the less you talk about Heaven and Hell, the more concerned you become with soup kitchens and equality and the more you find God present in all things—your fellow man, certainly, but also in the birds and the bees and the rocks and the trees.

Delahunty suggests that pantheism has a special attraction for democratic man because democratic man, like the pantheist, "has a natural bent to posit single, uniform causes behind complex and even contradictory events, rather than searching for multiple and varied causes that may include personal character and individual will."[46] Consider the notions of "progress" and "the sweep of history" and the idea of being "on the wrong side of history." Mankind has never been terribly comfortable with the radical freedom given to us by our Creator, and so he creates systems that explain away our freedom. Calvinism is such a system, as are various forms of determinism, Marxism, Freudianism, and indeed a pantheism that promotes everything from energy worship to radical environmentalism. These freedom-denying systems all wish to demote man to being no more than an animal—or even lower, a mechanical atomic machine—both in his biological makeup and in his moral worth, or lack thereof.

The most powerful bulwark against these soul-crushing faiths is the Rock revealed to us in the Bible and the Magisterium of the Catholic Church.

---

[46] Robert J. Delahunty, "Tocqueville on Pantheism: Part I," Law and Religion Forum, August 29, 2013, https://lawandreligion-forum.org/2013/08/29/tocqueville-on-pantheism-part-i/.

It is interesting that one of the main lines of attack against the Church is precisely over this question of freedom. The simplistic attack on the Church complains about the Church's prohibitions, primarily on sexual expression. But the Church is, in fact, the institution that most confidently proclaims man's freedom and his moral worth. It is precisely because man is free and important that what he does matters.

Therefore, what we are really seeing today is a drama that began with the rise of Christianity and continued as Christianity confronted and then supplanted the ancient pagan beliefs. Indeed, University of San Diego's Professor Steven D. Smith argues that almost all of the culture wars we have experienced starting in the 1950s can be understood and explained by this centuries-old battle between immanent religion and transcendent religion, between paganism and Christianity.

British writer Ferdinand Mount published a fascinating book ten years ago called *Full Circle: How the Classical World Came Back to Us*, in which he explores how "God's long funeral is over, and we are back where we started, 2000 years of history melted into the backstory, which nobody reads anymore. We have returned to year zero, A.D. 0, or rather 0 CE, because we are in the Common Era now, the Years of Our Lord have expired."[47] Mount argues the way we live our lives now bears a striking resemblance to the classical world, in our institutions, priorities, recreations, physics, sexual morality, food, politics, even religion, even if we do not know it. Anthony T. Kronman, former dean of the Yale Law School, has published a thousand-page opus called *Confessions of a Born-Again Pagan*. There is a fellow writing on social media

---

[47] Ferdinand Mount, *Full Circle: How the Classical World Came Back to Us* (New York: Simon & Schuster, 2010), introduction.

who says he is a pagan and calls himself Bronze Age Pervert. He has made such a splash that his *Bronze Age Mindset* was reviewed by Michael Anton at the *Claremont Review of Books*.

Nevertheless, one does hesitate to use the word *paganism*. It is a term easily dismissed. Technically speaking, the word *pagan* simply means "rural." The word was first used pejoratively by fourth-century Christians to describe those who kept the old gods. The keepers of the old gods were, at that point, country bumpkins from what we might call these days "flyover country." Today, rural people are, in fact, less likely to be "pagan" than Christian, and those we have called pagan would resist the term, though some who call themselves neo-pagan have embraced it. What's more, those we might call pagan now often live in the big cities.

To avoid these difficulties, in his book *Pagans and Christians in the City*, Professor Smith uses the term *immanent* rather than *pagan* to describe those who find the sacred in the material world, as pantheists do. Immanentists tend not to see beyond the material world. Even their energy worship is, in a sense, materialistic because their energy is perceived to be a part of this world — like magnetism or gravity — rather than outside of it. Immanentists may or may not believe in a life beyond this world, but they place the sacred, the things that ultimately matter, firmly in this world.

The ancient Romans were for the most part immanentists. While they lived in an enchanted, even god-haunted, world, their vision beyond the material world was limited. They may have believed their souls would travel to the underworld, but little was understood about this place. And the things that really mattered to them were found, for the most part, in the here and now, parceled out by the utterly capricious will of the gods.

It is also questionable whether their philosophers believed all the tales about the gods. It was largely something for the masses.

Ancients and Sex

The ancients were also obsessed with sex. In her book *Paul among the People*, Sarah Ruden provides a gruesome account of the porn-saturated world of the ancient Romans. Moderns are thrilled by the pornographic images on display at the ruins of Pompei; the Romans' interest in porn seems somehow to validate the contemporary obsession. Indeed, pornographic images were part of the warp and woof of ancient life. These images adorned the walls of homes throughout Rome. The male need for sex was called the "necessity." The male had free reign for sexual gratification from slaves, single women, and boys — though it was considered disgraceful to be on the receiving end of homosexuality. There were pornographic parades throughout Rome. Parents had to have their young sons guarded on their way to and from school so they would not be kidnapped and raped.

Ruden's book also explains why the emerging Christians were so hated by the Romans. It was not simply that Christians had an abstract and obscure theological belief in only one God rather than many, which is the story that is often told. It was also because they preached a profoundly different attitude toward human sexuality, one derived from their understanding of the human dignity conferred by God. The early Christians utterly rejected the wild sexuality of the Romans because it was dehumanizing. But the pagan Romans considered them sexual scolds. Sound familiar?

Professor Smith calls this battle over sexuality a Christian revolution. It raged for centuries, and in forms that are strikingly familiar to us today. Consider commercial activity. To engage in commercial activity, Christians were required to give divine honor to the Caesars. Without giving such honors, they could not gather the goods they needed to ply their trade. Without giving some kind of obeisance to the old gods, they could not work. Fast-forward to today. Walking down the streets of major cities, do you see rainbow decals in windows? Do you think every small shop owner displaying the rainbow symbol is a devout believer in "gay pride"? Or do you understand that many of them simply see this as the price of doing business. Czech writer Václav Havel recalls shop owners' displaying Soviet symbols in their windows, not because they believed in communism, but simply as the cost of doing business.

This will sound familiar to you. At certain points in the Roman-Christian conflict, public symbolism became extremely important. The most important symbolism was attached to public expressions of faith; and the expenditure of public money became a focal point of contention. As Professor Smith explains, political communities are at least in part "imagined." He says political communities are physical facts, certainly, but they also exist in the minds of the citizens. Therefore, symbols are vitally important to this imagining of community. The pagans and Christians certainly knew this. This is why the pagans vociferously objected when the Christian emperors of the fourth century cut off funding for the pagan temples and the vestal virgins. As British historian Edward Gibbon wrote, "The Roman sacrifices would be deprived of their force and energy, if they were no longer celebrated at the expense, as well as in the name, of the republic."[48] Ambrose, Bishop of Milan, argued that restoring the

---

[48] Edward Gibbon, *The History of the Decline and Fall of the Roman Empire*, 2:75.

money, even from past donations, would give imperial approval to pagan worship.

Roman temples littered the landscape of Rome and virtually every Roman city. But in the fourth century, most were destroyed, though many were converted to Christian churches. "The symbolism of displacement was starkly on display—as it was when Christian mobs, sometimes with imperial approval or at least acquiescence, destroyed the same temples," writes Professor Smith.[49]

Perhaps the most famous of these public symbolic tussles, a fight that went on for decades between the dying pagan faith and the rising Christians, was over the Altar of Victory. The altar is said to have been captured in 272 B.C. during the Pyrrhic War. It was installed in the Roman Senate house and was the site where senators burned incense and pledged their dedication to each new emperor. Quite obviously, the altar provided an undeniable link between church and state.

Christian emperor Constantius II had it removed in 357. It was restored by the pagan Julian but was again removed in 382 by Gratian. Influential men who still believed in the old gods continued fighting to have the altar restored to its place of prominence. Ambrose of Milan famously fought back. The ultimate Christian victory demonstrated who finally had the power in Rome. As Professor Smith put it, "In winning the fight over this and other symbols, Christians managed to create a conception of the city—of the 'imagined community'—as Christian, not pagan."[50]

---

[49] Smith, *Pagans and Christians in the City*, 175. During the short reign of Julian the Apostate, many of these new churches were razed and pagan temples built in their place. But this only further proves the importance of public symbolism.

[50] Ibid., 176.

Under Siege

We see these same fights today. A cross on a hill shows that we are a Christian people still, so modern pagans litigate to have it taken down. One of the sadder developments in this fight is that some of us have begun to argue that the cross, in these public spaces, is merely of historical significance. So we ourselves help to drain the cross of its real meaning. But even this is not enough for the new pagans. They know what the cross really means, and they know there is real power even in symbolism. So they will fight to take it down. Will we fight back?

In the fourth century, it may have seemed as if the fight between the pagans and Christians was finally over. It was not. It never will be, until the Second Coming. The pagans were simply driven out of the public square for a while. Now they are back with a vengeance.

5

Ours Is Not a Secular Age

The story told by the elite that this is secular age is quite frankly nonsense. Secular chattering takes place primarily in the postindustrial societies of the United States and Europe among high-status academics and those who have been spellbound by such academics. As you get beyond certain population centers, you find that the world is deeply religious.

This is true in Latin America, where many Protestant sects, primarily Pentecostalism, are exploding. This is true in Africa, where Protestant denominations and the Catholic Church are both growing tremendously. It is obviously manifest in the religious wars initiated by Muslims against Christians in Africa and the Middle East — and true also in the ongoing religious conflicts in India. Even the atheist state of China is suffused with religious conflicts. The notion that nonreligious secularism is everywhere galloping along is utterly false.

Nonetheless, because this idea dominates elite power centers, it demands our attention. This is especially true as it becomes more aggressive and seeks out heretics to punish. But it also requires our attention because there is clear evidence that Christianity is in some ways on a downward slide in this country and that the category of "nones" — those who no longer check the "Christian" box but rather say they have no religious affiliation — is growing at a hectic pace. Still, while the data on those not checking the "Christian" box can be alarming, consider this as you read of Christianity's decline: chefs reduce the sauce in order to intensify the flavor. Also keep in mind that nones are often not without religion. In fact, they are often intensely religious.

According to the Pew Research Center,[51] 65 percent of American adults now describe themselves as Christians. This is down 12 percentage points over the last decade. At the same time, the religiously unaffiliated continues to grow. Those who identify as atheist, agnostic, or nothing have reached 26 percent, up from 17 percent only ten years ago.

The Protestant denominations and the Catholic Church are experiencing similar declines. From 2009 to the present, self-identified Protestants have dropped from 51 percent to 43 percent, while self-identified Catholics have declined from 23 percent in 2009 to 20 percent today. At the same time, the numbers of so-called religiously unaffiliated have grown. Atheists are up from 2 percent in 2009 to 4 percent today. Agnostics are up from 3 percent a decade ago to 5 percent today. And the celebrated nones have grown from 12 percent in 2009 to 17 percent ten years later.

Pew says the nones are growing across all demographics: whites, blacks, Hispanics, men and women, in all parts of the country, among college graduates and those with lower levels of education. Pew says the nones are growing faster among Democrats than Republicans, though their ranks are growing among

---

[51] "In U.S., Decline of Christianity Continues at Rapid Pace," Pew Research Center, October 17, 2019, https://www.pewforum.org/2019/10/17/in-u-s-decline-of-christianity-continues-at-rapid-pace/.

Republicans too. While growth is more pronounced among young people, oldsters are succumbing to the lure of being "none." According to Pew, 2 percent of the silent generation have left Christianity, and 1 percent have become nones. Among baby boomers, 6 percent have left Christianity, and 4 percent have joined the nones. Gen X is down 8 percent in the Christian category and up 6 percent in nones. And then there are the millennials, who are down 16 percent in Christianity and up 13 percent among nones.

Putting aside percentages, raw numbers tell an even starker story. According to Pew, in 2009 there were between 176 million and 181 million Christians in the United States. Despite significant population growth, today there are only 164 to 169 million Christians.

Going back more than a decade tells an even more dramatic story. In the 1970s, self-identified Christians numbered 90 percent in our country. That is now down at least 20 percent. Protestants seem to have declined the most, from 64 percent in the seventies to 48 percent today. Catholics have dropped three percentage points from 26 percent to 23 percent in the same time frame, despite significant immigration. On the other hand, "no religion" has grown from 7 percent to 22 percent.

Digging deeper, the nones numbers tell a surprising story. They may be nones, but they are not nothing. They are not remotely "nothing." While 51 percent of them say they question traditional religious teachings, and 47 percent say they don't like positions that churches have taken on social and political issues — and 34 percent simply don't like religious organizations — interestingly, only 21 percent say they don't believe in God. Only 26 percent say religion is irrelevant to them. In fact, it is rather amusing to see in the Pew data that only 89 percent of atheists don't believe in God; and only 63 percent of atheists say religion is irrelevant to them.

All of this suggests serious doubt as to whether and to what extent nones are really nones. There is a great story about Louis B. Mayer, who told one of his producers that he wanted to make a movie about the Greek poetess Sappho. His producer said, "Boss, it'll be a movie about lesbians." "Don't worry," said Mayer. "We'll make 'em Americans." In this country, we can even make atheists into believers.

Nones, it seems, do not live in a godless world. In fact, their world is remarkably enchanted, enchanted with things like energy. Energy is very important to them, but so are spirits and even angels. Much of what follows is an examination of the do-it-yourself nature of American religion that will help demonstrate that, even now, we are a deeply religious people.

America has always been a land of religious entrepreneurs and do-it-yourselfers. How else to explain the likes of Mary Baker Eddy, who founded the Church of Christ, Scientist, and Joseph Smith, whose golden tablets inspired one of America's fastest-growing religions, the Church of Jesus Christ of Latter-day Saints, or Mormons? The nones and the agnostics and atheists are simply following the grand old American and Protestant tradition of protesting the prevailing religion and creating substitute faiths.

Consider an Iowan named Perry Baker, the father of yoga in America. It was sometime in 1889 when thirteen-year-old Baker met a traveling Indian yogi in Lincoln, Nebraska. How odd; how American! A Tantric yogi named Sylvais Hamati was holding events in Lincoln, Nebraska, in the late nineteenth century. Perry studied with Hamati for the next eighteen years. According to Baker biographer Robert Love, Baker learned the whole panoply of practices now familiar to soccer moms all over the country: the lotus position, breath control, the ritual cleansing of the body of toxins.

Baker eventually took the name Dr. Pierre Bernard and founded a school for yoga near Nyack, New York, north of New York City. His school attracted grand dames, industrialists, and many bold-faced names of the early twentieth century. They gathered like June bugs, flitting around Bernard's esoteric spiritual light. Baker did not create a new religion as Eddy and Smith did, but he franchised an old one and took it mass-market.

Have you ever heard of New Thought? It was huge in the nineteenth century and has reverberated down to the present day. New Thought was founded by a character named Phineas Quimby, who preached, among other things, that sickness originates in the mind and that right thinking can be the cure. Mind over matter, you know.

You can see New Thought in the work of Mary Baker Eddy, whose adherents avoid doctors because they believe they can cure themselves through mind control. You can see it in the work of Norman Vincent Peale and his *Power of Positive Thinking*. Peale married Donald Trump to his first wife at his Marble Collegiate Church on Fifth Avenue in New York. Trump still speaks of Peale's influence on his life. Napoleon Hill's New Thought book *Think and Grow Rich* was first published during the Depression and sold fifteen million copies. In many ways, Evangelical preacher Joel Osteen is a New Thought man. Americans may be spiritual gadflies, do-it-yourselfers, and religious entrepreneurs, but many are also rubes easily taken in by mountebanks. The religious need among us is so powerful that many try to find religious fulfillment in places that don't seem religious at all.

For example, the modern wellness and self-care movements that millennial nones have joined in droves are full of New

Thought—thoughts like selfishness. Indeed, wellness is perhaps one of the most self-centered movements of our time. It is about me looking better and me feeling better. It is almost completely inward looking. It does not seek to make the world a better place. It does not seem to have any kind of transcendent considerations. It is about the here and now and me, me, me. As the *New York Times* put it in 2019, "[Wellness] was a way to reorient ourselves—we were not in service to anyone else, and we were worthy subjects of our own care. It wasn't about achieving; *it was about putting ourselves at the top of the list that we hadn't even previously been on*"[52] (italics added).

Wellness is first and foremost a huge business. According to the Global Wellness Institute, Wellness is a $4.5 trillion market that includes $639 billion spent on Wellness tourism, $702 billion spent on healthy eating, nutrition, and weight loss—and a whopping $1 trillion on personal care, beauty, and antiaging products and services. Even Weight Watchers just rebranded to "Wellness Wins."

But wellness is also a religion, or at least a spirituality. Take a look at a wellness company called Goop. Founded by actress Gwyneth Paltrow, Goop is equal dollops wacky, unsubstantiated product claims, and spiritual lunacy. What started as a newsletter now commands $250 million in annual revenue, 2.4 million unique monthly visitors to its website, a magazine, a podcast, an annual conference, and an aspirational love letter from and to the lifestyle of the eponymous Gwyneth. When people say that

---

[52] Taffy Brodesser-Akner, "How Goop's Haters Made Gwyneth Paltrow's Company Worth $250 Million," *New York Times*, July 25, 2018, https://www.nytimes.com/2018/07/25/magazine/big-business-gwyneth-paltrow-wellness.html.

they are spiritual and not religious, something like Goop is often what they are talking about.

Consider the loopy products Gwyneth uses, such as Real Water with "E2 Technology" that "adds electrons to the water through electrical restructuring. The negative ionization can be measured in millivolts (mV) by an Oxidation Reduction Potential (ORP) meter."[53] Gwyneth's acolytes lap this up like mother's milk.

For $66 you can get a "Jade egg for your Yoni." *Yoni* is the Sanskrit word for "vagina." You are to insert it, and it will give you "joy and well-being." When not in use, you are to keep it in a "sacred space" that has "good vibes."[54]

And what of the crazy spirituality? Consider the "akashic-records healer" featured in one of the Goop summits. "She reads your past, present, and possible future," according to a clearly skeptical *New York Times* writer. The healer claimed to have flat feet because her feet had been chopped off in a previous life and whenever she's reincarnated, she comes back with flat feet because she likes the surety of her feet entirely touching the ground.[55]

On the Goop website you can find a lecture on self-love and another lecture about something called a "sound bath." There's a lecture from "intuitive" Dana Childs, who wants to be your "intuitive guide as we gracefully align with your Divine Blueprint." For the uninitiated, the Divine Blueprint refers to the "temples, power places and the global plan to shape the human soul." Google it.

---

53 Real Water product page, https://drinkrealwater.com/products/real-water/.
54 Jade Egg product page, Goop, https://goop.com/goop-wellness-jade-egg/p/.
55 Brodesser-Akner, "How Goop's Haters."

On the new Netflix show *The Goop Lab with Gwyneth Paltrow*, an energy practitioner hovers his hands over stressed-out clients in what a *Wall Street Journal* article correctly describes as "a spa version of an exorcism." The exorcist is a forty-seven-year-old body worker and chiropractor name John Amaral who charges upwards of $2,500 for a one-on-one session. He is seeking a trademark for his "Energy Flow Formula," which he claims can treat a number of illnesses.

His clients lie on an elevated table while he pants and moans as if intoning prayers. He sweeps his hands over and under them while they writhe and moan. Goop chief creative officer Elise Loehnen says that, while working with Amaral, she "had an exorcism."[56] During her session she retched and had dry heaves. She said, "Now people are really going to think I'm a witch."[57]

Amaral says, "I am not treating a particular condition when I am working with people but I have a hypothesis. If you just change the frequency of vibration of the body itself, it changes the way the cells regrow, it changes how the sensory system processes."[58] Amaral says the universe is made up of only 4 percent matter and the rest is energy, so we only have to plug into

56 Sharon Kirkey, "'I Was Like, Wait, No!' Did Goop's Chief Content Officer Really Have An Exorcism?" *National Post*, January 16, 2020, https://nationalpost.com/health/exorcisms-er -not-quite-but-netflixs-the-goop-lab-promises-other-what-is- happening-episodes.

57 *The Goop Lab with Gwyneth Paltrow*, Netflix, season 1, episode 5.

58 Anna Merlan, "The 'Energy Worker' Seen on Goop Has Im- plied That His Treatments Can Disappear Breast Cancer," *Vice*, https://www.vice.com/en/article/939kk8/the-energy-worker- seen-on-goop-has-implied-that-his-treatments-can-disappear- breast-cancer.

that energy. He says you can measure the energy field of each body from three or four feet from the body. The body does not end with the skin.

When he waves his hands over bodies, he says he is putting energy into the field of energy around them, changing their energy system. Often, his clients begin to moan and cry and convulse. He says he deals with people at the "sub-atomic level."[59] Dancer Julianne Hough says Amaral's work on her foot made her remember a traumatic period in her childhood.

At the Goop Summit, there was a reiki workshop, in which the practitioner had the faithful lie on the floor and share each other's energy. Energy is a big thing in modern-day spiritualities and is a tip-off that these are sublimated religious impulses. Energy worshippers may not believe in a deity beyond time and space, but they are anxious to connect to the energy that is all around them.

Two millennials from the Harvard Divinity School looked at a number of movements or communities that young people are joining in place of the local churches. Their paper tells the story of "How We Gather." The researchers say, "Overwhelmingly, these organizations use secular language while mirroring many of the functions fulfilled by religious community. Examples include fellowship, personal reflection, pilgrimage, aesthetic discipline, liturgy, confession, and worship."[60]

Note that millennials are suffering from an inordinate amount of loneliness, depression, and even suicide. The increasing isolationism of Internet culture contributes to this suffering. Although

---

[59] *The Goop Lab*, season 1, episode 5.
[60] Angie Thurston and Casper ter Kuile, *How We Gather: A New Report on Non-Religious Community* (Harvard Divinity School paper, April 2015), 7.

Internet culture can build community, it also encourages sitting in your room, alone, without immediate human contact.

SoulCycle is another mega brand that to outsiders seems an unremarkable exercise place with stationary bicycles, but to the initiated, it provides many of the benefits of faith. As Tara Isabella Burton writes in her important new book *Strange Rites*, "SoulCycle isn't just selling an exercise class for a weight-loss aide. It's selling a double ideal of purification: one simultaneously characterized by material improvement and by spiritual transcendence."[61] SoulCycle promises to "find your soul."

Classes, which start at $34 a pop, are not classes. They are "journeys," like pilgrimages. The Harvard Divinity paper reveals that instructors take on an almost pastoral role, very much like spiritual directors. The music played in the room is "liturgy-like." One SoulCycle devotee asserts, "God is a woman, and she's a SoulCycle instructor." The Harvard researchers say Soul-Cycle—now valued at nearly $1 billion—is one of today's most notable secular religions.

More than anything, it is a religion of the self.

Burton, who has written about this subject for years, says, "The implicit mantra of wellness is equal parts Ayn Rand and John Calvin: you're not just allowing but in fact obligated to focus on yourself—but, no matter how much you do, it will never be good enough."[62] Some say wellness is a moral obligation. They call it the wellness command.

Burton says the language of wellness, language about energy, toxins, "adaptogens," and neuron velocity, "is also about

---

[61] Tara Isabella Burton, *Strange Rites: New Religions for a Godless World* (New York: PublicAffairs, 2020), chap. 5.

[62] Burton, *Strange Rites*, chap. 5.

providing us with the sense of meaning, of order."[63] Finding a sense of "order" is an aspect of all religions. But what you will hear over and over in wellness culture is the word *energy*.

Certified soul coach and energy healer Jakki Smith-Leonardini says, "Everything is made of energy and has its own unique vibration, including you. Everything is in a constant state of receiving and radiating energy. The frequency of this imaging falls on a spectrum from light to dark. Light energy is infinite, effortless, and rooted in love. Dark or shadow energy is dense and rooted in fear. As an electromagnetic being, you attract experiences and relationships that match frequency."[64]

We are made of energy, and energy is all around us, and we will return to energy when we die. Does this not sound like a religious belief?

Burton points out that Americans are increasingly taking all of this energy talk very seriously. "A 2018 Pew poll found that a full 42% of Americans said they believe that spiritual energy can be located in physical objects."[65] This may seem similar to the Christian belief in the spiritual power of relics, but it is not. It is a belief that we come from energy, that energy is all around us, and that we will return to energy. This is more akin to the Eastern belief in the annihilation of the self.

One of the premises of our modern secularists is that religion is irrelevant to modern life; this justifies their efforts to exclude religion from the public square. However, it is impossible to

[63] Ibid.

[64] Jakki Smith, "About Energy Healing," Jakki Smith, https://www.jakkileonardini.com/aboutenergyhealing.

[65] Tara Isabella Burton, "How We All Became Jedis," Religion News Service, December 20, 2019, https://religionnews.com/2019/12/20/how-we-all-became-jedis/.

survey a landscape crowded with adherents to wellness, Goop, SoulCycle, energy practitioners, and a host of other New Age–channeling energy and vibration businesses without coming to the conclusion that the world is brimming with religious impulses, just as it has always been. The question is only which of these impulses should regulate our society.

Consider the startling growth of the occult in our supposedly secular world. In March 2019, Congresswoman Alexandria Ocasio-Cortez (AOC) shared her "birth-time" with a psychic, who then published the congresswoman's "birth chart" on Twitter. This horoscopus-pocus was a big deal for many. A "birth-chart" represents the positions and angles of the sun, the moon, the stars, and the planets at the time of someone's birth, organized into twelve houses: ego, sense of self; material possessions, security; local community, communications; home, family, and so on, and so on, and so tediously on. A writer at the fashion magazine *Allure* pointed out that AOC is "a Libra sun with an Aries moon" which is "a super powerful air-and-fire combo." All of AOC's "personal planets are either fire or air." This supposedly means AOC is "passionate and action-oriented, an idea-driven communicator with a strong grasp of intangibles."[66]

Back when newspapers were popular, you may remember having seen the horoscope. People might have read it and chuckled. They don't chuckle so much anymore. Horoscopes have grown far beyond that; they are much larger than you can imagine.

---

[66] Jeanna Kadlec, "Alexandria Ocasio-Cortez's Birth Chart, Explained," *Allure*, March 26, 2019, posted on Yahoo!, https://www.yahoo.com/lifestyle/alexandria-ocasio-cortez-birth-chart-205827662.html

According to Pew, 29 percent of Americans say they believe in astrology.[67] Only 22 percent identify as mainline Protestant.

But astrology seems quite tame next to witchcraft, which is also booming. Tara Isabella Burton says witchcraft may be the fastest-growing religion in America. Think of Rebecca Bratten Weiss, the former English teacher at Franciscan University of Steubenville. Weiss was let go from this Catholic school after her unorthodox views became widely known. She is online boasting about her grotesque witch fantasies, such as cutting the testicles off "Nazis" and burning them to a goddess named Hecate. She insists she is not a witch and that this was just a literary form. Former students in her circle, all connected to Steubenville, admit that they, too, have been influenced by witch culture.

Most of this is presumably intended, tongue in cheek, as a strike against "the patriarchy" of orthodox Christianity. Tara Burton argues that "for a growing generation of progressives(s), contemporary occultism—and modern witchcraft in particular—offers a powerful spiritual counterpoint to organized religion, one that's not merely orthogonal to traditional Christianity but actively opposed to it."[68] But that doesn't make its growth any less noteworthy.

Recall that occult favorite Marianne Williamson ran for the Democratic nomination for president and was welcomed as a serious candidate by the elite of the Democratic Party. Various researchers have placed the number of occult adherents at

[67] Claire Gecewicz, "'New Age' Beliefs Common among Both Religious and Nonreligious Americans," Pew Research, October 1, 2018, https://www.pewresearch.org/fact-tank/2018/10/01/new-age-beliefs-common-among-both-religious-and-nonreligious-americans/.

[68] Burton, *Strange Rites*, chap. 6.

roughly one million, more than Jehovah's Witnesses and almost as many as Episcopalians. #Witch at Instagram brings up more than eleven million posts.

During the Brett Kavanagh hearings, a woman named Dakota Bracciale led a gathering of witches to cast a spell on him. It is reported that ten thousand people registered for an event called "Hex Kavanagh." Bracciale owns an occult store in Brooklyn called Catland. She describes herself as queer and trans. The connection between the occult and sexual perversion is quite common.

Consider the thoroughly enchanted world of *The Angelic Experience*, a multimedia podcast, website, and in-person production of a rather spacy mother-and-daughter duo. They say they are "light-workers" who express the "opinions" of "Angels and Godly Presences." I am not sure precisely what this means, but they say, "The host lives are channeling these messages from much higher dimensions." I believe the two ladies are the "host lives."[69] This world can be a tad confusing. Catholics need no reminding that Lucifer was the most beautiful and luminescent of the angels. If they are really communicating with a higher presence, it's hard not to wonder which one.

All of this is wacky but also dangerous. We are called upon to discern spirits, and these spirits do not seem to come from above. Although most Americans self-identify as Christian, 60 percent of Americans report that they accept at least one New Age belief relating to spiritual energy, psychics, reincarnation, or astrology. It stands to reason that significant numbers of Christians believe in some of them, too. In fact, according to Pew, 47 percent of

---

[69] "About Lynn McGonagill," Lightworkers Healing Method, http://www.lightworkersmethod.com/LynnMcGonagill.html.

self-identified Catholics believe in spiritual energy in physical things, 46 percent believe in psychics, 36 percent believe in reincarnation, and 33 percent believe in astrology.

Again, what is abundantly clear is that the world of witches and New Age, Wicca, the Angelic Initiative, and even the Church of Satan are nothing if not utterly enchanted. One wonders if as many Catholics would have drifted away from the Catholic Church if the Church had spent more energy explaining traditional practices and beliefs such as the belief in guardian angels.

But of all the new religious groups, the sect interested in sex is by far the most prevalent. Anyone can perceive that our society is drenched in sex, obsessed with sex. Not surprisingly, sex permeates all the new denominations. As far as I can tell, none of them espouse traditional sexual practices. Rather, sex has become a sort of modern sacrament, one that is now managed by the state.

Historically speaking, sex obsession is nothing new. It is certainly not a product of the so-called sexual revolution. Throughout history, sexuality has been one of the elemental forces shaping our world. But American ingenuity has always expressed itself in peculiar ways, even with respect to sex. Did you know that even Oneida silverware company started as a sex cult? It was started by a preacher, no less, named John Humphrey Noyes, a graduate of both Dartmouth and Yale. He preached something called "perfectionism." He believed he was sinless and therefore could do all things. He may have been the coiner of the term *free love*.

Early feminist Virginia Woodhull called herself a "free lover" and declared that she had a constitutional right to have sex with anyone at any time, changing lovers daily if she wished.

She was a bit uncommitted, however: she went on to renounce her prior views and became what we would call today a "social conservative."

Of course, this was all considered strange and socially unacceptable in those days, except among a coterie of elites. But today it is Katy, bar the door. Noyes' and Woodhull's sex obsessions have become widespread.

My friend, Diana Kilarjian, lives in New York City and subscribes to an e-mail list of things happening in the city. In January 2020, this lovely Catholic woman was shocked to receive a notice about an event called Pass the Porn: A Cinematic Social Experiment—Altered States. It was billed as "an elevated and sophisticated version of that sleepover where one of your friends decided to search for porn and show the group. A cross between cinema and smut. Pillows, cuddle puddles, blankets and popcorn. And porn. Lots of porn."

The e-mail makes the rather remarkable claim that censorship is at an all-time high and that spaces to celebrate our sexuality safely are dwindling. They also claim that porn is not evil; rather it can be a force for good. They want to create a conversation around pornography and use it as a platform to "unpack" cultural nuances and norms. The event organizers certainly have norms of their own, such as a "zero tolerance policy for harassment, unwanted touch, homophobic, transphobic, racist, sexist, ableist, or ageist behavior." They even have what they call a three-second rule when it comes to creeping: you get three seconds to stare at someone; after that, it is creepy. Oh, and you can get an erection, but you are not allowed to use it.

On the very same day my friend received her city-happenings e-mail, another e-mail arrived promoting Kink Out: SPACES, an event at the Museum of Modern Art sponsored by Volkswagen.

Kink Out: SPACES is an "interactive and educational arena of kink/leather rituals, performances, presentations, screenings, and installations, including discussions of safe practices, healing, and activism." Religion-like ritual is a significant feature of this evening of sexual perversion.

So sex-obsessed are these fanatics that during the COVID lockdown, the City of New York made it a point to issue guidelines about how to keep it all going. The city issued a paper called "Safer Sex and COVID-19" that recommended sex with yourself, with someone you live with, or someone you know—but that if you do choose to go beyond that, to please keep the number as low as you can. And make sure there is consent. Consent is one of the highest sexual ideals.

At the New York–based New Society for Wellness, which is little more than a sex club tarted-up with New Age philosophy, they say, "Knowledge gained from expanding your sexual wisdom is one path to real happiness." They believe their members can gain "sexual enlightenment which will free them from the constraints of societal pressures to adhere to the additional relationships in sexual archetypes, allowing them to engage in stronger spiritual bonds with other souls." They had to close during the COVID lockdown. But they announced at the end of June that they were reopening with a class on something called *shibari*, which they eagerly explain is a form of Japanese bondage. One of the themes of the club is "kindness always matters."

Sex fiends are always *au courant*. Of course they have a Black Lives Matter initiative that seeks to "de-fetishize" skin color. It is a complicated sexual world. If you reject someone who is black, you are a racist. If you prefer someone who is black, you have fetishized them. They will need their own St. Thomas Aquinas to parse these difficulties.

A consistent theme of the sex-obsessed is the overthrow of both the family and the Church, both of which are seen as prisons where pleasure goes to die. This goal, and this understanding, both go back at least as far as the French Revolution. There is a profound revolutionary, even religious, fervor among the sex-obsessed. Tara Burton calls it a new theological system: "The willful defiance of a society that mandates repression and enforces heterosexual monogamy." Burton sees that they are sexual utopians who think that they will never be happy until they have broken free of the shackles placed upon them by traditional society. It is a deeply spiritual conception.

Julie Fennell of Gallaudet University in Washington, D.C., studied those involved in sadism and masochism and found that nearly half of the Americans and Canadians who engage in bondage and domination do so for spiritual fulfillment. One respondent told Fennell that "in the BDSM community you find a lot more spiritual people dealing with things such as energy or auras. Energy play or even things like astrology."[70] While most of this behavior provokes incredulity or disgust in normal people, it clearly reflects the need of its participants to couch their behavior in an aura of religiosity. They consider one unmentionably gruesome act as a "transcendental" experience.

This obsession with far-out sexual weirdness is widespread. The popular *Vanity Fair* magazine ran a story about the sex parties regularly organized in and around Silicon Valley, where wealthy tech founders and funders have their way with nubile young women, often facilitated by illegal drug use. The partygoers boast about their corporate efforts to disrupt business and society in

---

[70] Burton, *Strange Rites*, chap. 7.

the work they do; they claim to believe that these sex parties are producing similar beneficial disruption as well.

Our big-tech overlords have also subscribed to an entirely new transcendental goal, one they say will allow us to live forever—and not in heaven, but on this very earth. They dream of converting your consciousness into computer code to combine your humanity with machines that will never die. You may think that this is a joke, but they are quite serious. Major thinkers and funders and founders in and around Silicon Valley are deeply invested in this idea of transhumanism.

Ray Kurzweil received the National Medal of Technology and Innovation, the highest U.S. honor in technology. He also garnered $500,000 as the recipient of the Lemelson-MIT Prize in 2001. He has been inducted into the National Inventors Hall of Fame, which was established by the U.S. Patent Office. He has been honored by three U.S. presidents and received twenty-two honorary doctorates.

He is a very talented guy. But he is also barking mad. Kurzweil says we are connected to something he calls the "source," from which we came and to which we will return. He says, "What I have found is that there are different aspects of what makes up our consciousness. There are sparks of spirit that have experiences, and those sparks at some point re-join their source. That source doesn't have to be the only source, as that source that those sparks re-join may have another source, and so on. This is where such terms as the soul, over-soul and higher self come in."[71]

---

[71] Laron, "Ray Kurzweil Answers the Question, 'Do You Believe In God?,'" Transients.Info, September 22, 2016, https://www.transients.info/2016/09/7384/.

All this might be enough for a padded room if Kurzweil didn't work at the most powerful company in the world, Google. From that perch, he has been able to promote his concept of "the Singularity," the moment when machines will become smarter than humans and begin to run things. Kurzweil says we will be able to upload our neocortex to "the Singularity" and "we're going to be funnier; we're going to be better at music. We're going to be sexier. We're really going to exemplify all the things that we value in humans to a greater degree."[72] Kurzweil believes that in 2029 Artificial Intelligence will pass a valid Turing test and begin to show levels of intelligent behavior comparable to human levels of intelligence. He says, "I have set the date 2045 for the 'Singularity' which is when we will multiply our effective intelligence a billion-fold by merging with the intelligence we have created."[73]

Another Silicon Valley futurist, Anthony Levandowski, who helped invent self-driving vehicles, has founded a new church based on "the Singularity," which he refers to as the "transition." He says the event itself is going to be god, and that it is certain to make everything better. He is less sure about whether that god will be kind to us.

It goes almost without saying that Silicon Valley is almost universally anti-Christian. The HBO series *Silicon Valley* captures the mood well when the main character, who is hard at work reinventing the Internet, inadvertently outs a computer programmer as a Christian. He says, "You can be openly polyamorous

---

[72] Christianna Reedy, "Kurzweil Claims That the Singularity Will Happen by 2045," Futurism, October 5, 2017, https://futurism. com/kurzweil-claims-that-the-singularity-will-happen-by-2045.

[73] Quoted in Ed Lauder, "Ray Kurzweil Predicts That the Singularity Will Take Place by 2045," AI Business, March 17, 2017, https://aibusiness.com/document.asp?doc_id=760200.

and people will call you brave. You can put micro doses of LSD in your cereal and people will call you a pioneer. But the one thing you cannot be is a Christian."[74]

Wokesters

Silicon Valley futurists may be devoted to their strange gods. But another denomination has work to do here and now. The social justice warriors, the wokesters, are spreading like riot-fire.

Much has been written in recent years about the religious fervor of the movement that is bringing our country to its knees, both literally and figuratively. This Great Awokening, reminiscent of the Christian religious fervor that generated new American religious movements such as Pentecostalism, is now inspiring young people, black and white, to flood the streets, burn businesses, and beat the innocent.

Consider the recent video from a protest in Bethesda, Maryland, not far from where I live. Hundreds of white people are sitting on the ground, their hands raised in the air. A black man leads them in a liturgical prayer, "I will use my voice in the most uplifting way possible, and do everything in my power to educate my community. I will love my black neighbors the same as my white ones."[75]

---

[74] Quoted in Georgi Boorman, "Latest 'Silicon Valley' Episode Mocks California's Anti-Christian Animus," *Federalist*, April 19, 2018, https://thefederalist.com/2018/04/19/latest-silicon-valley-episode-mocks-californias-anti-christian-animus/.

[75] Emma Colton, "'Everything in My Power to Educate My Community': Protesters Recite Oath to Speak Out against Racism," *Washington Examiner*, June 4, 2020, https://www.washington-examiner.com/news/everything-in-my-power-to-educate-

There is the spectacle of white men and women kneeling in front of blacks, asking for their forgiveness. There are whites who go so far as to wash the feet of blacks. A Catholic priest said on social media that this was the natural inclination of people to confess their sins. William Faulkner said that slavery was America's Original Sin. But Faulkner is about to be canceled for his sins, and now the Left says that racism itself is America's "Original Sin." And unlike Catholics, who believe the effects of Original Sin can be addressed by Baptism, Wokesters believe that America's Original Sin can never be fixed. This is precisely the point: claims of racism can forever be used as a means to power.

Besides these hints of a belief in Original Sin, there are other traces of religion in the wokester creed. Certainly, there is confession. Even little children are asked to confess their racial sins. There is also damnation. Any transgression against the new faith can result in ostracism from polite society. People are fired from their jobs and shunned by friends, even their families, for supposed racial sins.

Consider the case of scholar Charles Murray, a well-respected Washington, D.C., intellectual who has published a shelf of well-regarded books. Many years ago, Murray published a book called *The Bell Curve*, which covered many topics, one of which was the question of whether there is a connection between IQ and race. For daring to examine the scientific data on this question, Murray has never been forgiven. One reviewer at the time said, "His book is just a genteel way of calling somebody a nigger."[76]

---

my-community-protesters-recite-oath-to-speak-out-against racism.

[76] Bob Herbert, "In America; Throwing a Curve," *New York Times*, October 26, 1994, https://www.nytimes.com/1994/10/26/opinion/in-america-throwing-a-curve.html.

A few years ago, Murray was invited to speak at Middlebury College in Vermont about his new book *Coming Apart*. The violent wokesters would not allow it. They began to chant religiously tinged slogans over and again. They turned their backs on him as if he were defiling their space. Eventually he and his host, Allison Stanger, were chased from the room and physically assaulted. Stanger has never fully recovered from her wounds.

Essayist John McWhorter, himself an African American, calls anti-racism one of our flawed new religions. He calls Atlantic writer Ta-Nehisi Coates a "new preacher" in this new faith. He says Coates's writings, particularly his tedious book on reparations, are cited like Scripture. McWhorter says the book is "quite simply, a sermon. Its audience sought not counsel but proclamation."[77] A more receptive reviewer said reading Coates is "essential, like water or air."[78]

As with any ascendant orthodoxy, there are questions that simply may not be asked. In the Middle Ages, one was ill-advised to ask certain questions about the Trinity. Now it is imprudent to ask why black lives seem to matter only when black men, often criminals, are killed by white police officers and not when they are snuffed out in the daily shootings among blacks in Chicago, Los Angeles, Saint Louis, and Washington, D.C. Even to ask this question violates orthodoxy and raises suspicions of heresy and racism. It is quite curious that only white sociologists and

---

[77] Quoted in Kyle Smith, "Black Critics Shake Their Heads at Ta-Nehisi Coates," *National Review*, September 21, 2017, https://www.nationalreview.com/2017/09/ta-nehisi-coates-black-critics-john-mcwhorter/.

[78] Quoted in Rod Dreher, "Reading Coates Is 'Essential, Like Water or Air,'" *American Conservative*, August 14, 2015, https://www.theamericanconservative.com/dreher/reading-ta-nehisi-coates/.

pro-family activists are talking about the catastrophic destruction of the black family that has occurred since the double blow of the sexual revolution and the 1960s' war on poverty. But to raise this question is again to reveal oneself as a dissenter and a racist.

In the days after the death of George Floyd in Minneapolis, the event that ignited riots around the country, funding for police forces was reduced. All around the country, a significant upsurge of inner-city murders followed. Hardly a whisper of concern was heard from Black Lives Matter and other "social justice" groups.

Refusing to "take a knee," a practice initiated by football mediocrity Colin Kaepernick, is to place oneself outside of the new faith. NFL quarterback Drew Brees expressed praise for the American flag and was made to recant and apologize. He has apologized several times, in fact, but they still want more from him.

Leftist journalist Michael Tracey speculated, "Among the reasons why this still amorphous 'movement' became so widely popular with such break-neck speed is perhaps because in the eyes of many it transcends mere politics. Many so-called protests took on features highly reminiscent of religion: collective worship, public confession and requests for salvation, devotional poses and gestures, group prayer, creation of a new pantheon of martyred figures to revere, and the adoption of liturgical rites and rituals."[79]

Tracey goes even further and calls this a new state-backed religion because government officials have not only stood aside while Black Lives Matter destroys towns but have, in fact, knelt or shown other forms of obeisance to the new faith. For example,

---

[79] Michael Tracey, "Black Lives Matter is a state-backed religion," *Spectator*, June 25, 2020, https://spectator.us/black-lives -matter-state-backed-religion/.

at a Caldwell, New Jersey, high school, students persuaded a police detective to sing the national anthem for their Black Lives Matter demonstration while "legions of suburban white women in yoga pants knelt with their fists raised finally to the sky."[80]

But finally there is sex again, always sex. Remember when Larry Summers, short-term president of Harvard University, was dismissed for speculating about why women hold fewer tenured positions than men in science and engineering at elite universities and research institutes? Even raising the question violated the tenets of social justice, intersectionality, and woke. Likewise, Google employee James Damore was fired after he speculated why there were more men than women at places such as Google.

In this chapter, I have tried to show that claims of secularity by the religious Left are largely false and that the death of religion is greatly exaggerated. The nones and all their co-religionists may think they are secular and scientific, but their worldviews are undergirded by faith just as all worldviews must be. They do not want secularity in our politics or in our government. What they want is for government to establish their own new faiths, as our English forebears once did, and declare other faiths, most explicitly Christianity, as heretical. They want an established State Church of their own.

[80] Ibid.

6

Live Not by Fear

The crises in our world and in our Church are so immense, so myriad and manifest, that many people turn away in fear or despair. Others lose themselves in nostalgia. Still others squander their time in entertainment. Each of these temptations can lure us away from the tasks God has given us and distract us from living fully and robustly in these desperate but glorious times. Be not afraid! There are halos hanging from the lowest branches of the trees.

Fear

Rod Dreher is a well-known conservative writer with a popular blog and a series of successful books. He and I were friends long ago in New York City, though we parted company during the Long Lent of priest sexual abuse revelations in 2002. I thought he overplayed it, and this caused a rift between us that has never healed, though I later admitted in print that he was right, and I was wrong. But fear seems to animate Dreher. Given his large audience, it seems quite possible that he has frightened hundreds of thousands of Christians and conservatives nearly to death.

Many of Dreher's fears are understandable. When Islamic terrorists attacked Manhattan, he could see the towers burning from his Brooklyn neighborhood. Even so, his fear sadly got the better of him: he concluded that New York was too juicy a target, and that it would happen again. So he abandoned the city.

Shortly thereafter came the Long Lent of ecclesiastical sexual abuse. Dreher reported on this for years. Alas, like Lot's wife, he peered too closely and for too long at the evil, and the fear got to him. Though he said he left the Catholic Church for many reasons, including that he came to doubt some of the Church's claims, he also said he left because he was afraid for his sons.

But Dreher is clearly drawn to an apocalyptic and fearful frame of mind. In 2006, the "peak oil" scare hit the news. Plenty of experts maintained that we were nearing the peak, and that the inevitable decline of fossil fuels would follow just as the demand for them was skyrocketing. Lloyd's of London agreed; so did the Royal Institute of International Affairs. A year later, Dreher reported that the world had already reached peak oil and that civilizational disaster loomed.

What happened? Oil production in the United States did drop precipitously from roughly nine million barrels a day in 1985 to roughly five million in 2007, and global demand did increase precipitously. But then, oil production took off like a rocket, largely because of the production process known as fracking, which has turned the United States into the largest oil producer in the world. We now produce approximately twelve million barrels a day, not to mention a great deal of natural gas. Our fossil-fuel-based civilization is not ending anytime soon.

Twelve years later, the coronavirus began marauding across the globe, taking lives and leaving devastating economic ruin in its wake. It is understandable that Dreher was afraid. As he wrote, "I don't have any marketable skills that don't involve writing. I have a mortgage, and kids. Poverty, and all the insecurity that comes with it, frightens me too. I'm old enough to remember my father's stories about his rural Depression childhood. I'm not that far removed from poverty, historically."[81]

And yet, the virus produced more than just rational anxiety. It seemed to satisfy a deep need for end times. Eight years ago, Dreher's "Why We Love Apocalypse" reflected on the 9-11 attacks, saying, "The world was clear and crisp and full, in a way that it hadn't been before." He said it was a kind of high. I remember that, too. On the day of the attacks, there were fighter jets screaming overhead, cars were stopped on city streets, doors were open with radios blaring the news as crowds listened anxiously. But Dreher finished his thought this way: "It is deeply ironic that for many of us, the only thing worse than apocalypse is the thought that we are condemned to muddle through."[82]

But are apocalypse and muddling through the only two options? What about joy and a fighting spirit? We were made for this, after all, made for times of trouble. God Himself has called us to this time, not to any other, and not, it seems, to a time of ease and comfort. God sent the likes of us. As Winston Churchill said during the Second World War, this is a great hour to live.

But all this is mere preamble to Dreher's vision of the soft totalitarianism we are facing with the Supreme Court's *Obergefell* decision and the inexorable calamity that will befall practicing Christians. It is here that Mr. Dreher eases from fear to despair.

---

[81] Rod Dreher, "Of Poverty and Crooked Hearts," *American Conservative*, March 27, 2020, https://www.theamericanconservative.com/dreher/poverty-crooked-hearts-middle-class-coronavirus-christianity/.

[82] Rod Dreher, "Why We Love Apocalypse," *American Conservative*, December 21, 2012, https://www.theamericanconservative.com/dreher/why-we-love-apocalypse/.

He maintains that we have lost the Culture Wars and that all that is left for us is to hunker down until the new dark ages are over. Just as the Benedictines kept culture alive when the soil went bad, intentional Christian communities must protect their children from contamination, preserve Christian culture, and live to fight another day. It is unclear whether Mr. Dreher believes another day will dawn. But in the meantime, he preaches a sort of withdrawal — tactical withdrawal, but withdrawal nevertheless — from the poisonous and predatory outside culture. We should become, in his words, "exiles in our own country."[83]

Dreher is not alone. There are many others, and their fear feeds upon itself. My friend Joe Sciambra, former homosexual, has spent recent years trying to wake up the Church and explain how churchmen have been complicit in the confusion about human sexuality, specifically homosexuality. He recalls Catholic priests' encouraging him in his homosexuality and his open gay life. He was looking for a life preserver, and the priests he met gave him an anchor. He spends his time at homosexual events, handing out rosaries and telling the men that Jesus loves them. But he sees active gay parishes all over the place in San Francisco, Los Angeles, and New York, and he cannot get a hearing from the local bishops. He is in despair. I fear he will leave the Church. I admire Joe Sciambra immensely, but he seems to have forgotten Mother Teresa's admonition that we are not called to success but rather to fidelity.

Catholic pundit Steve Skojec also seems close to despair. In a moving cry of the heart published in September 2020 called "No

---

[83] Rod Dreher, "American Exiles," *American Conservative*, June 26, 2015, https://www.theamericanconservative.com/dreher/american-exiles/.

More Platitudes," he wondered why he fights for the Church. He says the Church is his entire identity but that the problems seem so immense as to be almost insurmountable. He asks, "What do we do when time and again, we are confronted with the unthinkable? What happens when the pope himself—THE POPE HIMSELF—says contraception is OK, or approves Holy Communion for people living in adultery, or changes the *Catechism* in a way that reverses the Church's infallible bi-millennial teaching on the moral liceity of the death penalty ... or signs an interfaith document that undermines the exclusivity of salvation through the Church?"[84]

He condemns Paul VI for allowing changes in the liturgy and wonders why Pope Paul was raised to the altars. How could this have happened? Paul VI ushered in the most "destructive period in the internal life of the Church in history."[85] He talks about spineless bishops, wanton sexual abuse, and ideological and moral scandals throughout the Church.

It seems to me that Skojec is in a kind of despair because, after a lifetime of fighting, his whole life, so he says, has come to nothing. He has not won. Things have only gotten worse. He has only known a Church in crisis. When may we rest in the joys of the Faith and not have to fight?

It makes perfect sense that, reading Skojec's column, Rod Dreher would find an ally in doom. Rod says he was happy to make Skojec's acquaintance because, later on, when we are all in prison, we will need each other. Rod is thinking about the

[84] Steve Skojec, "No More Platitudes: It's Time to Take a Hard Look at the Crisis of Catholicism," OnePeterFive (blog), September 15, 2020, https://onepeterfive.com/no-more-platitudes-its-time-to-take-a-hard-look-at-the-crisis-of-catholicism/.

[85] Ibid.

gulag and sharing blankets and perhaps pieces of bark for food, maybe escaping and making the long trek through the Rocky Mountains to the Pacific Coast and then take leaky boats to Free Siberia, or something like that.

But I say no. I see all the same threats that Dreher and Skojec and Sciambra and many others do. They are indeed frightening. But we cannot, we must not, give in to our fears. Where they say retreat, I say, "Into the breach, charge and always with a smile in your face, a spring in your step, and joy in your heart." They may accuse me of offering platitudes, of being a Pollyanna. But despite the devastation all around us, I do see amazing bright spots, moments of grace, great hope, and also the great honor of having been called at this time to take up the Cross, as they would have said during the Crusades.

I am put in mind also of the early Christians living in the dominant pagan culture that from time to time viciously persecuted them. I think, too, of the generations of people who were born, lived, and died while the Arian crisis raged. They all knew dark times, as dark as and darker than ours. But they did not give in. They did not despair. They embraced their age and the struggles God brought them to, and they did it with great joy.

They are teaching "transgenderism" to the public-school children right down the block. Should we say, that's too bad, but our task is not to fight it? That our task is to organize like-minded groups of families to homeschool, attend our own churches, create our own art, set up a quiet yet competing public square, and to hell with those public-school kids who very well may come knocking on our doors to ask our daughters out? What the retreatists do not recognize is that there is no withdrawal or tactical retreat from the dominant culture. They are here.

As I wrote in *Crisis Magazine* in 2015, "Do you remember Chick-fil-A Day and all those long lines of Christians standing up for the principle of free speech and Biblical marriage? Remember how amazing that was and how the LGBT lobby was weeping copiously over their blog posts? They were in full panic mode. They had no idea we were so big."[86] The response to the bigotry and power of the gay lobby was not to shrug and go back to making our own chicken sandwiches; it was a massive action in which faithful Christians lined up for hours at Chick-fil-A restaurants all over the country to fight back by buying food.[87]

The proper response to the desperation all around us, the proper response to challenges and even persecution, is not tactical retreat until the dark age finally passes, but joy that God has called us here now to defend His creation. As former education secretary Bill Bennett has said, "We are a 'let's roll' people, not a 'let's roll up in a ball' people."

Nostalgia

Fear and despair are not the only temptations in these dark days. There is also nostalgia, golden-age thinking, daydreams that squander our time and draw us away from the tasks God has set before us.

This kind of nostalgia comes in many forms. The wistful wishing that you had been born at another time and place is common.

---

[86] Austin Ruse, "Corporations Are the Enemy," *Crisis Magazine*, March 13, 2015, https://www.crisismagazine.com/2015/corporations-enemy.

[87] Some will argue that Chick-fil-A ultimately caved under pressure, when their management changed. But the primary point is unchanged.

Under Siege

I am looking at a photograph that shows all the altar boys who served at a particular time in 1950s Philadelphia. There appear to be more than a hundred of them all lined up in their cassocks, not a ponytail among them and certainly no sneakers peeking out from under the robes. Wouldn't it be wonderful to have lived then?

I am looking at another photo of the New York City skyline taken during Easter 1956 and can see three skyscrapers, including the Chrysler and Empire State buildings, lit up with crosses. These days New York skyscrapers are lit up with rainbow colors to celebrate homosexuality during "pride" month.

How easy it is to be nostalgic for those days when it seemed as if everyone practiced or respected the Faith. It is easy to be nostalgic for a time when the cardinal archbishop of New York could command the attention of the city and the governor. From 1934 to 1968, the Hays Motion Picture Production Code governed the content of our movies. This code was created by Catholics. Think of that kind of power. It is the power sexual deviants now have.

Rather than the 1950s, others may muse wistfully about the Middle Ages. How wonderful to have lived under a benevolent Catholic king, they think, with thriving guilds, working your own plot of land, bursting monasteries nearby, torchlight processions marching through the streets. Life may have been harder than it is now, and life expectancy much shorter, but the Faith would have been so easy, maybe even magical. (Just don't think about the medicine or the hygiene.) Hilaire Belloc may have been channeling this sort of thinking with his economic "distributism," which required that everyone own land, or at least a piece of the company where they worked, and not simply be wage slaves to capitalist masters.

Writing in the *Catholic Herald* in the summer of 2019, Matthew Schmitz called this "Lost Worldism." Others have called it

Golden Age Thinking. Schmitz says, "Anyone who has had the misfortune of spending much time among brainy right-wingers will have heard someone say, 'The only government I could support is the Habsburg Empire', or 'Politics has become impossible since the rise of the nation-state. We must return to the reign of Louis IX', or 'The only worthy political venture on the continent died with the conquest of Catholic Quebec'."[88]

Schmitz points out that even the revered figure Alasdair MacIntyre, the inspiration for Dreher's *Benedict Option*, had fallen for Lost Worldism. In his book *Dependent Rational Animals*, MacIntyre argues that the common good "can be realized neither in the forms of the modern state nor in those of the contemporary family." For models of the common good, he points to small fishing communities, Welsh mining towns, farming cooperatives, or "some city-states from a more distant past."

Schmitz says correctly, "When I imagine a better world, I refrain from building castles in Spain."

But one group of Catholic men whose influence is felt down to the present day tried to do precisely that, at least metaphorically speaking. They were led by Brent Bozell Jr.,[89] one of the most interesting figures of late twentieth-century America. His

---

[88] Matthew Schmitz, "Longing for lost worlds won't convert America," *Catholic Herald* (UK), June 13, 2019, https://catholicherald.co.uk/longing-for-lost-worlds-wont-convert-america/.

[89] Brent Bozell Jr. was the father of Brent Bozell III, head of the Media Research Center and a frequent commenter on the political and media scene. Brent Bozell's grandfather was a PR maven. From Omaha, Nebraska, he named Boy's Town. The movie of the same name was his idea. And he founded what became Bozell Worldwide, among the largest public relations and advertising companies in the world.

life and times are masterfully told in *Living on Fire: The Life of L. Brent Bozell Jr.*

Bozell and his colleagues, particularly Frederick Wilhelmsen of the University of Dallas, were so enamored of Spain in the 1960s, they decided to host, under the auspices of their *Triumph Magazine*, an annual student summer program at El Escorial, the ancient home of the Spanish kings. Just outside Madrid, El Escorial is only a short drive from the magnificent monument the Valley of the Fallen, hewn out of a mountain by Francisco Franco to honor the war dead of the Spanish Civil War. The so-called Benedict Option, a strategic gathering into like-minded communities of faith, predated Dreher by several decades.

The summer programs were highly influential. Many students who participated went on to important positions in the Catholic world back in the United States. In fact, out of these *Triumph Magazine* summer programs grew Christendom College, which thrives to this day in Front Royal, Virginia. Dr. Timothy O'Donnell, an alumnus of those long-ago summer programs, is the head of the college.

Bozell took the summer programs further than any of his colleagues. Rejecting what he saw as the flawed Enlightenment founding of the United States and appalled by the Protestant materialism he saw metastasizing at midcentury, Bozell moved his young family to Spain in 1965 to live in the shadow of El Escorial amid the gloried past of the Spanish Catholic monarchy. He said that in Spain "you breathed the Catholic thing."

Bozell and his colleagues were not Francoist or fascists or Falangists, or members of any of the other more pungent parties present in Spain starting in the 1930s. But they were of the Carlist party—that is, they believed the Spanish monarchy must be restored through the Bourbon family, specifically through the line of Don Carlos, Count of Molina. One of Bozell's attractions to Francisco Franco was his commitment to restore the Spanish monarchy, which Franco eventually did. There are echoes of this kind of nostalgia in Catholic circles today.

To his credit, Bozell did not remain in Spain. He returned eventually to the United States. Indeed, he came back and ran for Congress. He did have a fighting spirit. Bozell founded perhaps the very first U.S. pro-life group, called the Sons of Thunder. They dressed like Carlists, in khaki clothing, with red berets, images of the Sacred Heart across their shirts, and crosses hanging around their necks. They must have been a sight to behold when they invaded the abortion clinic near George Washington University in December 1970. Bozell himself slugged a policeman with a five-foot cross, for which he was prosecuted. A writer for a local Washington, D.C., paper called the demonstration "the most ludicrous Defense of the Faith [*sic*] since the Fourth Crusade diverted their holy enterprise to the raping of Constantinople."[90]

Brent Bozell saw in the Spain of the 1960s what he considered to be an authentic Catholic culture, one less afflicted by the consumerism of postwar America. But he eventually succumbed to manic depression, ending his days as something of a holy fool flitting around the United States and the world on quixotic Sancho Panza crusades until his disease finally got the better of him and he died, without a doubt, in the odor of sanctity.

What we find in Bozell is the seed of more than one of the nostalgic tendencies found among contemporary Catholics to

---

[90] Lester Kinsolving, "Rumblings from the Sons of Thunder," *Free Lance-Star*, December 12, 1970, 5, https://news.google.com/newspapers?nid=1298&dat=19701212&id=j2YQAAAAIBAJ&sjid=XooDAAAAIBAJ&pg=2583,2435556.

this day. From debates about monarchy to "integralist" discussions about subsuming American government to the Holy See, they are temptations to take us away from the real work God has given us to confront the ongoing societal crises in our lands and our times.

Golden-Age Thinking

Bozell's legacy is clearly visible in the sometime humorous debates some Catholics have about monarchy. As comedienne Rita Rudner once joked, "Neurotics build castles in the air. Psychotics live in them. My mother cleans them."[91] The modern-day monarchists must know in their hearts that their musings are fanciful. And many monarchists, though not all, are quite jolly indeed.

Michael Warren Davis, my friend and former editor at *Crisis Magazine*, is a delight, as is Charles Coulombe, a man I hugely admire and a fellow writer at *Crisis*, who argues that our king, the American king, would be Franz Herzog von Bayern, Duke of Bavaria, head of the House of Wittelsbach, because he is in the direct line of the Catholic Stuart kings, who were overthrown and eventually excluded from the British crown for their Catholicism. He has written a what-if history—*Star-Spangled Crown: A Simple Guide to the American Monarchy*—about the monarchy returning to these shores. Noted military defense writer William Lind, who has also been deeply involved in the culture-war battles of the past quarter century, holds that the

---

[91] Quoted in Carla Baranauckas, "Rudner Is Firmly Rooted and All Over the Place," *New York Times*, August 31, 2006, https://www.nytimes.com/2006/08/31/arts/31rudn.html.

old Prussian monarchy is the way to go. He says, "Of course, like all real conservatives, I am a monarchist." His attachment is to the House of Hohenzollern.[92]

I sometimes interact, and am indeed friendly, with a religious association called the American Society for the Defense of Tradition, Family and Property that endeavors to keep alive the various royal houses around the world. In the pro-life movement, I have worked with the descendants of many royal houses in Europe, such as Duke Paul of Oldenburg, who lives in Brussels and fights the culture war with me and others. But these descendants of royal lines do not clamor for the restoration of the houses their families lost along the way. They see that there is real work to be done.

Perhaps there is some gallows humor among the monarchists that is designed to keep the spirits of the troops up. Or perhaps it is of some small use to examine other forms of government. Indeed, some of their observations about the current system are hard to refute. As Coulombe has reminded us, St. Thomas Aquinas described "three kinds of good government—Monarchy, Aristocracy, and what they called 'Polity'—that is to say, rule by an educated, landholding, and military-serving citizenry." Opposed to each are "Tyranny, Oligarchy, and what they called 'Democracy'—mob-rule." St. Thomas Aquinas and Aristotle believed the best form of government would be a mix of "King, Nobility, and landholding, service-minded Commoners."[93]

92 William S. Lind, "Military Matters: When the West Died," United Press International, October 27, 2006, https://www. upi.com/Defense-News/2006/10/27/Military-Matters-When -the-West-died/81311161952812/.

93 Charles A. Coulombe, "Are You a Monarchist?," Tumblar House, December 16, 2019, https://www.tumblarhouse.com/blogs/news/ are-you-a-monarchist.

But there is clearly a strong element of parlor-game nostalgia among the monarchists.

Integralism

And then there are those Catholic intellectuals and academics who muse about integralism. Integralists argue not just that the state must be informed by Catholic thinking but, at the extreme, that Catholicism should be the official state church. Here, too, Bozell's legacy is apparent. Some even take this to its logical conclusion and support the political persecution of Protestants.

Bozell came to believe that America was badly, and perhaps irreparably, founded on Enlightenment ideas and that our current troubles are the inevitable result. He believed that the United States could be made right only by a Catholic refounding. But this harsh critique of the American Founding starts to sound anti-American, and indeed it was the cause of Bozell's eventual break with his colleague and brother-in-law William F. Buckley Jr. Nevertheless, Bozell's arguments are still made today by influential Notre Dame Professor Patrick Deneen, who has a growing following among young Catholic men. Professor Deneen is close with Rod Dreher.

Integralism came to the forefront of public discussion recently when *First Things* magazine published a defense of Pope Pius IX's taking a Jewish boy from his family home and into his care, much against the will of the boy's parents. It seems the boy had been baptized by a Catholic servant when the boy was sick and was therefore Catholic and could not be raised in a Jewish home and must be raised in the Faith. These were the Papal States, and the law of the land required it. The issue became a *cause célèbre* in the United States and is a scandal to this day.

The *First Things* article concluded, "It is a grievous thing to sever familial bonds. But the honor we give to mother and father will be imperfect if we do not render a higher honor to God above.... Should putative civil liberties trump the requirements of faith? We should be grateful if that question does not become pressing, but we cannot assume it will not."[94] The article by a Dominican professor at Saint John's Seminary in Boston launched an ongoing debate about a confessional state.

No less than Harvard law professor, and recent convert, Adriene Vermeule and *New York Post* opinion editor Sohrab Ahmari, also a recent convert, are involved in the debate about liberalism and religious freedom. Ahmari is a brave, happy warrior. He initiated a great debate about Drag Queen Story Hour and how classical liberalism is congenitally unable to deal with this affront to women, children, the family, and the Faith. Ahmari argues that local government should have the power to prevent drag queens from parading half naked in front of toddlers because such behavior is offensive to Christian values. By contrast, classical liberals such as Protestant writer David French argue that Drag Queen Story Hour defends the virtue of our current system: because drag queens get to do their thing, therefore we Christians will be able to do ours.

I remember quite well hearing these thrilling debates more than twenty years ago when I spent years with and among the traditionalists of the indult Tridentine Mass in New York City. In those days, "integralism" was used less than the phrase "the Social Reign of Christ the King," a doctrine from the popes circa 1880–1925 that had been long forgotten but was revived by Mr.

---

[94] Romanus Cessario, O.P., "Non Possumus," *First Things*, review of *Kidnapped by the Vatican*, by Vittorio Messori (February 2018), https://www.firstthings.com/article/2018/02/non-possumus.

Bozell, his colleagues at *Triumph Magazine*, and later iterations of Catholic traditionalism. The Social Reign of Christ the King does not require a monarchy. It requires only that men and governments recognize Christ's Kingship over our lives. There is plenty of warrant for this from Pope Leo XIII and Pius XI; there are beautiful encyclicals that I commend to you.[95]

But as interesting as they are, debates about monarchy, distributism, integralism, and the Social Reign of Christ the King have about them the smell of the faculty lounge, the graduate-school dorm, and breakfast bull sessions after the Sunday Tridentine Mass. They also provide fodder for the leftist mainstream press to say, "Look what those crazy, scary, nutty Catholic intellectuals are up to now." These ideas will never travel far beyond the tony intellectual precincts where they thrive. Rather, these siren songs of nostalgia turn the Catholic layman away from the difficult work of engaging our actual society as it actually is. We will never be ruled by a king. Catholic ideas will never explicitly rule the United States government. The typical person will never move to a small farm or fishing village.

Distraction

Put aside fear; do not let it freeze you into inaction. Put aside academic debates about integralism and nostalgic arguments about monarchy. Consider the most widespread temptation that takes us away from what is happening in the world and stifles our proper reaction. It is distraction. We live in the most distracted

---

[95] See Leo XIII, *Rerum Novarum* (May 15, 1891); Piux XI, *Quas Primas* (December 11, 1925) and *Ubi Arcano Dei Consilio* (December 23, 1922).

era the world has ever known. Right there, you looked down at your phone, didn't you? Or you did a minute ago. It is hard to read even a page of text without checking e-mail. I know a holy priest who has to leave his smartphone in the rectory because he is tempted to check it during prayers. We must check to see what's new on Facebook. We must get back to that Twitter war. We must check the box scores to see how our team is doing. Late into the night, we must binge on the latest television series.

Quite simply, we are distracting ourselves to death — perhaps even to perdition. I was tempted to say we are *entertaining* ourselves to perdition, but this really isn't entertainment. It is distraction. And it has profoundly dangerous consequences not just to us and to our family life but to society as a whole.

When the local grade school is teaching kids that sex is assigned at birth and that boys can be girls, the response of most is: I think I'll go play golf or watch TV. Have you ever wondered why escapist fantasies are so popular in books, television, and movies? The Marvel series, the *Star Wars* saga, *Game of Thrones*, futuristic series such as *Westworld*, and apocalyptic shows such as *The Walking Dead* take us out of our day and time and deflect us from considering the real-world crises all around us.

At least the monarchists are arguing about the important issue of how we should govern ourselves, and the benefits of alternative systems. At least monarchist Charles Coulombe contributes important observations to the debate, such as the fact that no monarchy has imposed abortion or same-sex "marriage" on anyone anywhere. But the mass of people who chose fishing on Sunday over the Holy Mass, who are stuck to their iPhones and home screens — they are missing the chance to participate in one of the most glorious times in the history of the world to be a faithful Catholic.

Under Siege

In the twelve months ending 2017, Americans spent $100 billion on sports alone. We spent nearly $40 billion on movies and another $20 billion on music. According to the Nielson audience-measuring company, Americans devote upwards of ten hours a day to screen time. The U.S. Department of Labor tells us that men spend nearly five hours every weekday on leisure activities, including sports, and more than seven hours on the weekends. Women are not far behind.

There are only so many hours in the week—only 168, in fact. The workweek takes up roughly forty hours. If you get seven hours of sleep a night—that is, if you are not binging *The Walking Dead*—you have forty-nine hours of sleep. Three hours a day may be taken up with eating, bathing, dressing, and preparing food—that's twenty-one hours. Know what's left over? Fifty-one hours. That would be plenty of time to volunteer for a cause. Except that we spend fifty hours a week on screen time: checking e-mail, looking at Facebook, warring on Twitter, and so much more. Of course, much of that is spent when we should be working. But you get the point; we spend an ungodly amount of time with our noses in screens.

Where the Romans had bread and circuses, we have *Game of Thrones* and countless other programs from what many call the Platinum Age of Television. Consider the intense attention millions devote to March Madness. Even the phrase needs no explanation. Everyone knows March Madness. President Obama made his picks, and it made national news. Notice, too, that the Super Bowl is now treated as something of a national holiday. One wonders how many hours upon hours are wasted watching men playing with various kinds of balls.

No wonder most folks say they really don't have time to go to that meeting, make a few phone calls, or sit down and study an issue. No wonder no one has the time to delve into what they are teaching the kids at the local grade school. Most folks think they don't have the time to write a letter to the editor or reach out to the local school principal.

And then consider that in 2019, when the local school board in Fairfax County, Virginia, debated radical new policies on human sexuality, including telling first graders their sex was selected at birth and can change, about fifteen people showed up to protest. Such a dearth of interest is played out in school districts all over the country where children are in danger and men and women are distracted by modern bread and circuses.

So many halos and so many crosses are ignored because we spend so much time distracted. I'll say it again: those who devote so much time to their entertainment are likely to miss the grand sweep of our time; they are likely to miss it altogether.

Lastly, there is something called "self-sufficiency," the belief that you cannot do anything since you cannot fix it yourself. This is a kind of modern Pelagianism that asserts that our societal problems are so immense, there is nothing you can do. This, too, is a kind of despair and evinces a lack of faith, since we are never acting on our own but always with God's help.

There is another way. There is another course beside the paths of fear, nostalgia, and distraction. There is a life filled with joyful fighting spirit and the realization that God has placed us here from the beginning of time to be His heroes. At the beginning of this book, I promised that I would show you the straightforward pathway out of the abyss. It is time, finally, to start our ascent. Follow me now, and let me show you the way.

7

No Finer Time to Be a Faithful Catholic

This is a time for rejoicing! It is as joyous as any time in the life of the Church. How blessed are we to be here now when everything seems so lost! How blessed are we to be called by God to defend His creation right here, right now. Our Father in Heaven knew this battle would be upon us. He knew these times would be desperate. In His providence, He allowed these desperate times. He knew His most blessed creation—the human person—would be attacked. And yet, He sent us, you and me, to fight this battle. We are as blessed as any generation of Catholics who have ever been called to defend Holy Mother Church.

William Gavin writes that "the radical Left, in every country in which it has gained power ever since the French Revolution, has wanted to dismantle, destroy, marginalize, or make impotent the Roman Catholic Church."[96] And make no mistake: most, if not all, of our society's deadly aggression is aimed at the Catholic Church. The Church is the only institution that has stood solidly against the agenda, and now the religion, of the sexual Left. The

---

[96] William F. Gavin, "Obama, Athanasius, and the Bishops," *National Review*, February 15, 2012, https://www.nationalreview.com/corner/obama-athanasius-and-bishops-william-f-gavin/.

Church has never wavered even once on abortion. The Church has never wavered even once on marriage and the family. The Church, while not seeking to impose her teaching on any man or woman, has provided a prophetic witness to the dangers inherent in contraception. And the Church is the world's leader in proclaiming and defending freedom of religion. Consider, by contrast, that abortion, contraception, and sexual perversion are all sacraments of the sexual Left, and now of the established State Church. The Catholic Church stands against all of them.

Faithful Catholics even today are fighting for the soul of our country. They fight to defend who we are as Americans. They fight also to defend the Body of Christ.

Those of us who understand the fight and who engage in it are relatively few. And our opponents are vast and rich and powerful: the federal government and all its terrible might, the mainstream news media, rich men and women, rich foundations, the entertainment industry, and powerful nongovernmental organizations, including the federally funded billion-dollar-a-year baby-killer called Planned Parenthood. One could faint dead away if one focused too closely on our desperate situation. But remember, Gideon's army was tiny too, only three hundred men. God seems to like giving us long odds. It forces us to remember to give Him the glory, when we succeed.

But there is other good news, too. We are promised by our Faith that God can bring good out of any evil.

What good, you might ask, could God be bringing out of the long-standing attacks on the unborn child and the attacks on marriage and the family? What possible good, you may wonder, can come from the exponential growth of human sexual perversion? What good can God bring out of the current government-initiated attacks on freedom of religion?

Perhaps the great coming together of His children.

What we have seen over the past quarter century is something we have not seen since the great rupture of Christendom during the Protestant Reformation. If God grieves, one can imagine that the grief of that split might be the greatest of all, for He wants His children to be one.

What we have seen over the past quarter century is the great coming together of God's Christian children. Catholics and Evangelicals are putting aside theological and ecclesiological differences. We are banding together to fight back against the State Church. We are fighting together to protect the unborn child, to protect marriage and family, and indeed, to protect the right of each of us to practice our faith in our own way.

Ecumenical initiatives, such as Evangelicals and Catholics Together, have brought together distinguished public intellectuals, such as Catholic Professor Robert George of Princeton and Evangelical hero Charles Colson. The Manhattan Declaration, a statement of common principles, was signed by more than six hundred thousand Evangelicals, Catholics, and even Jews and Muslims. But it is in the trenches, in front of abortion clinics and on the steps of state capitals, where the bonds of pew-sitting Catholics and Evangelicals have been forged, fighting together for marriage and children.

In my own pro-life and pro-family work at the U.N., I work closely with Evangelicals and those of other faiths. We see a war against God's creation, and all God's children must work together to protect His creation. We care equally for the Catholic mom, the Evangelical dad, and the Muslim child who are all trying to resist the pressure brought to bear by powerful U.N. agencies, wealthy Western nations, and billion-dollar foundations. It does not matter to us that our brothers in this fight are from other faiths. During the Beijing +5 women's conference at the U.N., in the wee hours before the conference started, I invited Mormons and Muslims to a secret exorcism said by a Catholic priest on the balcony of the huge U.N. negotiating hall. It was incredibly moving.

In our ecumenical coalition at the U.N., I point out that what we all have in common is that we are all strong believers. Many faithful Catholics find that we have more in common with hard-nosed Calvinists than we do with dissenting Catholics. I am proud to work with those who believe I am not only theologically wrong but *damnably* wrong, and I would have it no other way. I can count on a strong believer, even one who believes differently than I do. You can't really count on someone who professes Catholicism but then rejects its foundational teachings.

Make no mistake about it: God wants abortion to end. He wants the slaughter of the innocents to end. He wants marriage restored in the way He made it. He wants us all to be able to discover Him and proclaim Him, free from interference and coercion by the state.

But He wants just as much as all of these things for His children to be one and, eventually, to be with Him in Heaven.

This is not a call to indifferentism. It is not to say that all roads lead to God. I am a faithful Catholic, and I believe the Church is not just the one true Church but, really, the only Church. And I am not afraid to say that to my brothers of other faiths in this fight. In fact, I once told a room full of senior Muslim diplomats that God wants all of them to become Catholic. I also told them I was there to help them with their conversion. They sat there and grinned from ear to ear. They appreciate those with strong convictions and brave faith; they have that, too, for their own faith. But in the present fight, we must put aside our disagreements and fight against a common enemy that is coming for us all.

If we do this right, we know what will happen. I have seen it with my own eyes. We will grow closer. We will become friends. Understanding and sympathy will grow. Love will appear like those little flowers in the front yard when spring comes. This is the true ecumenism; people of strong faith working on common projects and letting love grow. And we have much to learn from each other. Evangelicals are no longer relying exclusively on Scripture to make their case. They are becoming increasingly conversant in natural law philosophy and the Catholic approach to public argumentation. At the same time, Evangelicals are teaching Catholics how to evangelize others in our Faith. We are more courageous in speaking in expressly religious terms. We are more courageous in citing Scripture and in publicly proclaiming our Faith.

I believe that we, as Catholics, owe a debt of gratitude to our Evangelical brothers and sisters for proclaiming the faith bravely in the public square, on television, and even on the street corner. I recall that my own conversion was deeply influenced by listening to Evangelical street preachers in Farragut Square in Washington, D.C. I used to listen to them during my lunch hour in the early 1980s and marveled at their bravery in taking on all comers. This kind of thing has kept the faith boiling in this land, and it may be the thing that saves us in the end. And the Catholic Church's unwavering witness to the sanctity of human life, and the defense of the unborn child and the natural family, has proven remarkably attractive to those seeking the ultimate truth.

So, this burgeoning relationship is one of the great goods God has brought from great evil. The other quite amazing thing that has happened in the past few years is a great awakening of our Catholic bishops. In our current crisis, this may ring of false praise. After all, there is widespread apostasy, and we do not see the bishops universally standing strong; many of them are careerists who want only to achieve that inviting red hat. Others are likely cowards who do not have the stuff to stand up to the State Church and simply want a quiet life.

But consider this. When John Kerry—a dissident Catholic—ran for president in 2004, George Weigel told me that "no more than thirty-five" bishops could be counted on to speak out publicly about Kerry's dissent from Church teaching on abortion. And Weigel was exactly right. That was a pitiful number of the nearly two hundred shepherds of Christ in America, even taking into account the Church's fears about losing its donor-benefiting nonprofit status. But a few years later, when President Obama was invited to speak at Notre Dame and to receive an honorary degree, that thirty-five grew to eighty bishops who spoke out in opposition.

But then came the great attack on our religious freedom with the compulsory coverage of contraception, especially abortifacient contraception, mandated by Obamacare. Every single bishop who leads a diocese in the United States, more than two hundred in all, condemned it. The bishop's unanimous objection is unprecedented in modern times. Moreover, this objection was not an obscure memo written by a layman and issued from some committee of the U.S. Conference of Catholic Bishops; it came in individual announcements from individual bishops who were willing to stand for this most controversial truth. Many of the bishops vowed to go to jail rather than comply with this unjust law. I rather wish some of them had. What a glorious witness that would have been.

Consider also that this opposition came in the midst of the priest sex scandals, when so many bishops were accused of protecting perverted priests and mishandling the complaints of victims. As William Gavin writes, "Who, after all, would have believed the Catholic bishops, old, celibate men, their authority weakened by the manner in which they dealt with the homosexual sex scandal, scorned by the major media, not listened to by the vast majority of Catholics concerning the Church teaching on contraception—who could imagine that these ... people would say "No!" not once but twice to the president of the United States!"[97]

The commitment of those in religious vocations and consecrated religious life is increasingly vibrant. But these are not the only measure of Church health. There is also lay engagement. And for lay engagement, we are living through a quite remarkable time.

Consider how God organized the Church. There are a tiny number of bishops, a larger number of ordained priests—and billions of laymen. What this means is that if we are to subdue the world for God as He wishes, we cannot rely strictly on the ordains. We must do our job as well. After a speech I gave years ago in Ireland, a little old lady came up to me and said, "What you say is all well and good, but I am going to wait for the bishop." No. We do not have to wait for the bishop. We should not wait for the bishop. We have our own warrant from God Himself. We do not need the bishop's approval to do our jobs. He doesn't even want us to ask him. He wants us to act. I told this anecdote at another speech, and afterward Cardinal Bevilacqua of Philadelphia came up, shook my hand, and said this was exactly right.

Now, some will scoff that lay involvement is not new. They will point out that there was a more robust laity in the 1950s;

---

[97] Gavin, "Obama, Athanasius, and the Bishops."

churches were packed; Corpus Christi processions paraded through the streets; and there was little dissent. All this is true enough. But I have often wondered why all that collapsed in the 1960s. Some point to the sexual revolution. That is certainly a contributor. Others wonder if it was Vatican II that caused the collapse. Perhaps that had something to do with it. But Vatican II is the seminal event of the Church in our age, and because of that, understanding it is like the proverbial attempt to see a mountain while living on the side of it. Only time and distance will give people some perspective. Our hope can be that our descendants will have a better view of the mountain and will be able to comprehend it.

I also wonder if the Faith of the fifties was a bit too rote, that not enough of it was internalized. I wonder if we relied too much on our priests to be holy and catechized, so that as long as they were, then we were fine and did not have to make the Faith our own. When the storm came, we discovered that our faith was built on sand.

When I began to consider conversion to the Catholic Church in the late 1980s, I approached young people I knew to be Catholic and asked them what I should read. Not one of them could make any recommendations. Not one. This was the first great uncatechized generation in the Church. But we must assume that their parents, who came of age in the great 1950s, were not catechizing their own children. We must conclude that priests who were of mature age in the 1950s were not catechizing these kids either.

Put that aside for a moment and consider what I had to do to convert, and how good it was. I had to find the Faith on my own. I had to find the sources, the books, and the teachers on my own. This, of course, was dangerous. I was blessed in knowing that I could not knock on just any parish door. After all, the priest answering might not have given me the true Faith. So, I found the Faith in odd places: in the novels of Anthony Burgess, in James Joyce's *Portrait of the Artist as a Young Man*, in the movies *Amadeus* and *The Name of the Rose*. I do not recommend any of these, but they worked for me. Consider that in *Amadeus*, Salieri hated God. Nonetheless, he believed in God intensely, so much so that he wanted to destroy God's creation, Mozart. These odd sources drew me closer to conversion. And then the wonderful event: I discovered Ignatius Press, and I knew that everything that they published would be solid.

Two things to consider: First, I had to make the Faith my own. I had to dig the marrow of the Faith out of pages of books no one gave me, books I had to find on my own. This is one of the great developments of our time. Our Faith is no longer rote. It must be internalized. It must be made our own. We must fight for it. What a great blessing! Second, note where I found the Faith. The priest who finally received me said he had never met a person who had "read his way into the Church." But I think it is quite common these days. I, and many others, find the Faith preserved and presented by Catholic publishing houses that are largely run by laymen.

It's true that Ignatius Press was founded by a Jesuit, Fr. Fessio, but it has always been run by laymen. And Ignatius is not the only one. Sophia Institute Press was founded by layman John Barger. St. Benedict Press, a private company that purchased the failing TAN Books, is run by the Charlotte-based Gallagher family. Cluny Press is in the business of reprinting great Catholic classics. Angelico Press is run by my old friend John Reiss out of his home. Imagine, there was a time when the lay-run Catholic publishing industry was a desert.

Turn to broadcasting. Look at EWTN, founded by a nun but always run by laymen. It now reaches a worldwide audience. There is also Salt and Light Television, based in Canada. And there are now hundreds of Catholic radio stations—Guadalupe Radio, Relevant Radio, EWTN radio—whose "voice goes out through all the earth, and their words to the ends of the world" (Ps. 19:4).

Catholic colleges and universities are exploding. Wyoming Catholic is established in the wilds of the Rockies and encourages its students to bring their own horses! Orthodoxy is alive and flourishing at Belmont Abbey College, Benedictine College, Christendom College, Franciscan University of Steubenville, Magdalen College, Thomas More College, and the University of Dallas. There is a hard core of orthodoxy at the University of Notre Dame, a school that could have been lost. Orthodoxy has also been revived at the Catholic University of America; it was a hard slog back from the radicalism of the 1960s.

Consider new initiatives such as the Thomistic Institute, created by the Dominican House of Studies in Washington, D.C., which now has chapters on more than thirty campuses around the country. There is the Love and Fidelity Network, a student-run pro-life and pro-family group that is on more than a dozen campuses, including those of the Ivy League. FOCUS, a student evangelization group, is active on hundreds of campuses in forty-eight states.

There are new lay initiatives in the new media, such as Taylor Marshall's, which has several hundred thousand paying customers. There is OnePeterFive, started by Steve Skojec partly to call out what he sees as the corruption in the Church, up to and including the papacy; there is also Where Peter Is, started by D. W. Lafferty to defend Pope Francis. There is *Crisis Magazine*, where I am a regular columnist, and also *Catholic World Report*, the *National Catholic Register*, and on and on. Note that these are all lay initiatives.

Remember Pope Leo XIII's 1884 vision of the devil betting God that he could destroy the Church if he were given the twentieth century? Satan certainly did great damage to the world and to the Church too. But those hundred years were up in 1984. How many of these initiatives germinated in the final years of the twentieth century? There are no coincidences.

Prolific Catholic author Mike Aquilina sums it up: "I'm ancient enough to remember a time when there was no 'Catholic publishing' to speak of, when there was no Catholic TV. Now these platforms are thriving — and dominated by the laity. Who would have predicted a time when our universities were turning out so many lay theologians? If priests have gone silent because of thinning numbers and institutional pressures and workload, the dogma speaks loudly nonetheless — perhaps more loudly than before."[98]

The central message of this book is that there has never been a finer time to be a faithful Catholic. Not the fourth century, not the thirteenth. Now. How could this possibly be? First, because all of us are so very badly needed. Not even a single one of us can be spared. The problems are so immense and there are so few of us: what a blessing it is to be here now. The good Lord has given each of us specific talents and specific tasks to carry out. These tasks were ordained for us from the beginning of the world. If we do not carry them out, they will fall to another or more likely will go undone. And so it is left to us, to faithful Catholics, to work at our tasks and at those that others have abandoned.

It is not *in spite of* the manifold and manifest problems in society and the Church that makes this the finest time to be a

---

[98] E-mail conversation with the author.

faithful Catholic but precisely *because of them*. God called us here now, when He knew the societal collapse would come. He called us here now, when the Church would come under attack. You say we are not equipped to go up against the State Church, that we do not have the stuff to fight those who went to Harvard and Yale and now occupy the heights of power in culture and the law and the media. I say, who cares? Where is your sporting spirit?

At the U.N., where I have spent twenty-four years fighting just this kind of elite, every time my colleagues and I walk into the room, we can sense the growing anger of our betters. They laugh at us. They mock us. They try to keep us out. But over the past quarter century, we have stopped them from making abortion a global human right. We stopped them from redefining the family. We succeeded in negotiating a proper definition of gender. Oh, how they hate our little ragtag band of Christians who have bested their betters time and again for all these years. Even showing up at a meeting makes things better. They say that those who make history are those who go to the meeting and stay to the very end. Many a long night at the U.N., when negotiations would end with the sun rising over the East River, one could look into the gallery and see that the only ones still there are this ragtag band of Christians. It is glorious work.

I travel all over the country and the globe, and wherever I go, I see catastrophes. But wherever I see catastrophes, I also see faithful Catholics striving to fix them. Whether it is defending the Faith or defending the faithful, good Catholics are there.

Did you know that our own Catholic Church administers more hospital beds than any other institution in the world? The homosexual elite may hate the Church and her teachings, but Catholics care for more AIDS patients than any other institution in the world. Not even Catholics know this.

Even in setback, there is honor. It was Catholics such as Robert George of Princeton and Maggie Gallagher, then of the National Organization for Marriage, Brad Wilcox of the University of Virginia, and Ryan Anderson of the Heritage Foundation who led the intellectual fight to save traditional marriage. They weren't the only ones. There were many others. But it was Catholics who led the way.

It is our own Church that has been the lone institutional bulwark standing up for the unborn. On the day *Roe v. Wade* was handed down, the Southern Baptist Convention issued a statement praising the decision. Imagine that. The Catholic Church is protected from this kind of error. Our Church has never wavered on the issue that Pope St. John Paul the Great called the most pressing human rights issue of our time.

You want to make a difference? Grab a broom. When I was a kid, I worked in fast food. The boss would say, "You got time to lean? You've got time to clean." How true is this today. Turn off the TV, drop that game console, forget the daily box scores. God will ask you about none of that. Do something. Do anything. Do not live in fear or nostalgia or avoidance.

St. John Paul the Great called each one of us to be among these defenders of the Faith and of the faithful. During the whole of his magnificent pontificate, his central message to young people, indeed, to each of us, is that we must strive for greatness of heart and never settle for mediocrity. The great Richard John Neuhaus put it well when he said we must dare to live the high adventure of Catholic orthodoxy.[99] Isn't that a remarkable statement? St.

---

[99] See Richard John Neuhaus, "The Catholic Center," *First Things* (April 2003), https://www.firstthings.com/article/2003/04/the-catholic-center.

Josemaría Escrivá said each of us must have a sporting sprit. The sporting spirit means you want the ball. You want to take the shot. You want to score the goal. This high adventure, this sporting spirit, means more than private piety, going to Mass, saying your Rosary—though it means these things to be sure. It means participating in the public struggle. This is a cup that none of us should forgo. We are enjoined to preach the gospel to the whole world.

Saints

We have lived in a time of great saints. We need not long to have lived in some distant age, an age when we imagine that great saints and spiritual giants lived. We live there now. So, if you are asking yourself, "How can I fight this immense evil?" take your inspiration from our own great saints and spiritual giants. Did you know they have been all around you? Our present age can compete with any age for great souls. Perhaps you have not thought about this. Or maybe you have simply forgotten. I am here to remind you.

Consider that people in the Middle Ages may not have realized that they lived in a time of great saints. After all, they did not live in a time of mass communication. The saint in one diocese would have been unknown to the layman only a few miles away. Today we can take courage from saints from all over the world. We know about them right away.

We have lived in the age of Padre Pio, the Capuchin friar who needs no introduction. You already know that he had the Stigmata and that he could read souls. You may even know he had the power of bilocation. Imagine, we have lived when he lived.

We have lived in the age of Mother Teresa, who founded a global congregation of sisters who care for the poor. You are aware that Mother lived many years of her life with no spiritual consolation. Yet she persisted and showed us the way to manage hard times. This great gift is given to only the greatest of saints—to walk through the shadow of the valley of death without even a glimmer of hope. And we lived when she lived. Many of us met her.

Consider St. Josemaría Escrivá, who founded Opus Dei, a global Catholic apostolate with ninety thousand members and the first personal prelature proposed by the Second Vatican Council. He died in 1975. He is of our time.

And then there is Gianna Beretta Molla, a medical doctor who refused medical treatment, and sacrificed her life, to avoid harming her unborn child. Her daughter lived. I have met her. There is hardly a community of Catholics anywhere in the world without a healthy number of girls named Gianna, the name of my own daughter. St. Gianna Beretta Molla died in 1964. She was beatified in 1994 and canonized ten years later. We lived in her age!

There are countless others. Have you heard of Ven. Montserrat Grases, a teenager who gave all for Christ? Or the teenager Bl. Pier Giorgio Frassati, the handsome mountain climber who died in the odor of sanctity?

Pope St. John Paul II bestrode not merely the Catholic world but the entire globe as a mighty colossus. Millions gathered to catch a glimpse of him, to hear him speak, to be close to him. He is already colloquially called "the Great." One day, he will bear the title officially and will be a Doctor of the Church. We lived in his age. We saw him. We touched him.

Martyrs

In preparation for the Jubilee Year 2000, St. John Paul the Great issued an apostolic letter "On the Third Millennium," wherein he predicted a great springtime of the Faith heading into the new millennium.[100] We can take comfort from his foresight. But he also entreated the Church not to forget the flood of Christian blood that flowed from the twentieth-century martyrs, for we have lived in the bloodiest century of martyrdom in the history of the Church. We should take great strength from their witness: the blood of the martyrs has been recognized as the seed of the Church since Tertullian made the observation in 197.

Inspired by St. John Paul's entreaty, a small group of Catholic laymen in Connecticut began to collect the stories of twentieth-century martyrs. Their efforts grew into a vast global project; stories of martyrdom poured in from all over the world. Dr. Robert Royal of the Faith and Reason Institute in Washington, D.C., was given access to the files stored in offices of the Commission for New Martyrs on the island of Isola Tiberina in Rome. He compiled them into a book called *The Catholic Martyrs of the Twentieth Century*.

Consider Armenia. In 1915, 1.5 million Armenian Christians were murdered by the Ottoman Turks. This included 7 bishops, 126 priests, and 47 nuns. Some say this is a drastic undercount.

Consider China. Royal reports that millions of Christians were murdered for their Faith during the Chinese Boxer Rebellion in 1900. To this day, Chinese Catholics are persecuted by the Chinese Communists.

Take Mexico. In 1917, the Mexican revolutionists drew up a socialist constitution, the first in the world, predating even the Soviet constitution. It included several articles meant to destroy Catholicism. In his fine novel *The Power and the Glory*, Graham

---

[100] Pope John Paul II, apostolic letter *Tertio Millennio Adveniente* (November 10, 1994), no. 18.

Greene wrote movingly about a Mexican priest who traveled around, in constant fear for his life, administering the sacraments. Many real priests like him were put to death. In the Jubilee Year 2000 Pope St. John Paul II canonized a group of twenty-five who were murdered during the Cristero War. Visualize Miguel Pro lined up against the wall with his arms outstretched just before the bullets ripped into him as he shouted, *"Viva Cristo Rey!"* The Mexican Communists demanded that a fourteen-year-old boy named José Luis Sánchez renounce his Catholic Faith. He refused. A priest recounts, "Consequently they cut the bottom of his feet and obliged him to walk around the town toward the cemetery. He cried and moaned with pain, but he did not give in. At times they stopped him and said, 'if you shout, "Death to Christ the King" we will spare your life.' Jose Luis finally died shouting 'Long live Christ the King' while his assassins fired upon him."[101] We have lived during the age that this brave young martyr lived. It should embolden your heart to know that you lived in his era.

Then there is the Soviet persecution. According to Royal, 200,000 Catholics disappeared in the eight years between the Bolshevik revolution and 1925. He says that by 1925, the number of Catholic priests in Russia had fallen from 245 to 70. An entire community of Dominican nuns was kidnapped by the Soviets; where they went has never been ascertained. Persecution of Catholics throughout the Soviet Empire continued through much of the twentieth century. Many great men and women refused to betray Christ, paid the ultimate price, and received the martyr's crown.

---

[101] Quoted in "Viva Cristo Rey!," Catholic Tradition, http://www. catholictradition.org/Saints/cisteros1.htm.

During the Spanish Civil War of the 1930s, priests and nuns were shot down in the street. Churches were burned. Convents were burned. There is the famous photograph that captures the moment: a line of Republican troops firing their weapons at a statue of Christ. In fact, the majority of the twentieth-century martyrs beatified by St. John Paul II were from the Spanish Civil War. Before the Jubilee Year 2000, among the 266 beatified, 218 were Spaniards, including 3 Discalced Carmelites, 26 Passionists, 8 Brothers of the Christian Schools, 71 Brothers Hospitallers of Saint John of God, 51 Claretians, 12 Scolopi religious, 17 Sisters of Christian Doctrine of Mislata, along with several bishops, various diocesan priests, members of religious orders, and laymen and laywomen.

But there was more, plenty more, bloodshed in this bloodiest of the Church's epochs.

Picture a row of men on their knees, lined up on a Mediterranean beach, their hands tied behind their backs. Each is wearing an orange jumpsuit. Behind each kneeling man stands another man, dressed in black from head to toe, each brandishing a huge butcher knife. The men in orange, all Christians, were led like lambs to the slaughter. With macabre choreography, the men in black pushed their victims' faces down in the sand and beheaded them. The Islamic killers filmed this most brutal act of martyrdom. Their film shows Christian blood mixing into the waves of the sea. Dr. Matthew Mehan, dean of the Hillsdale College graduate program in Washington, D.C., is an expert on martyrs. He informed me that one of the orange-clad victims was actually one of the executioners. In the instant before the atrocious act, he switched sides. Imagine. We lived when this man lived.

Gruesome events like this have been repeated across the Muslim world. Churches have been burned with hundreds of

Christians inside. Christians have been hunted and slaughtered for their Faith.

On July 26, 2016, Fr. Jacques Hamel celebrated Mass at the altar of his church near Rouen, France. Two Islamic terrorists approached him, and he exclaimed, "Go away, Satan."[102] They cut his throat.

Little Suffering Souls

The martyrs of our age have given spectacular witness. But many others have suffered for their Faith as well. I have written extensively about three young children I call the "Littlest Suffering Souls": Brendan of Great Falls (1997–2013), Margaret of McLean (1993–2007), and Audrey of La-Celle-Saint-Cloud (1983–1991). These modern children, children of our day, suffered greatly, died young—and brought many to the Faith. Each, in my view, is a canonizable saint.

Two weeks before his death at sixteen, Brendan Kelly's aunt helped him into bed one night. He was a big boy, weighing more than two hundred pounds, and massive steroid treatments to fight the ravages of chemo had weakened him so much that it was difficult to get him into bed. It was even more difficult because large sores covered his whole body. There was no place he could be touched that did not hurt him—except his head. So his aunt patted his head, and Brendan said, "Aunt Kelly, I am so happy. All you need to be happy is to open your heart to Jesus."

---

[102] "'Go Away, Satan,' French Priest Declared before Being Killed by ISIS Terrorists," *National Catholic Register*, https://www.ncregister.com/news/go-away-satan-french-priest-declared-before-being-killed-by-isis-terrorists.

Under Siege

Suffering on and off with leukemia for years, Brendan sometimes suffered with depression. Asked by his psychiatrist what that was like, Brendan retorted, "It's like driving a car with Karen in the back." Despite his pain and suffering, Brendan had a great sense of humor: Karen is a reference to one of Brendan's favorite movies, *Talladega Nights*, about a racecar driver named Ricky Bobby whose father put a panther in the back seat of his racecar so Bobby would overcome his fear of driving fast. This boy with leukemia and Down syndrome had an encyclopedic knowledge of this movie and the television show *The Office*. And he loved Jesus. The psychiatrist eventually stopped charging for his visits because "talking to Brendan is like talking to God."

Brendan had a sixth sense when it came to pain in others. A friend of his sisters came from an abusive family, and the girl was full of sadness and even hate. She was mean and uncommunicative. Brendan became her holy nuisance. He sat with her, put his head on her shoulder, talked to her, tried to make her laugh, and insisted that Jesus loved her. This went on for weeks. She hated it. But eventually she cracked. She smiled and laughed—and was transformed into a new person.

Brendan treated his suffering in the distinctively Catholic way by joining his suffering to Christ and thereby helping others. When Brendan was fourteen and undergoing a bone marrow transplant, as they drew out his bone marrow, they heard him telling Bella Santorum he loved her. They could hear him offer his suffering for this child of Senator Rick Santorum who was born with Trisomy 18, a condition doctors say is "incompatible with life." To this day, the Santorums credit Brendan with saving Bella's life. Bella, who was not supposed to survive her birth, and who was considered a candidate for abortion, turned twelve in the spring of 2020.

Peter O'Malley, a banker friend of Brendan's father, got caught up in a terror attack on a hotel in Mumbai. He hid out for hours to avoid the killers who were targeting Americans. Peter made two phone calls, one to his company's security team and the other to Brendan, asking for his prayers. Later that night, Brendan wandered into his father's dark office and said, "Jesus told me Mr. O'Malley will be rescued today." He was.

Brendan was a mystic. He carried on a nearly constant conversation with Jesus and with his guardian angel. After Confession one night, he carried on an extended penitential prayer. Outside, his father asked what took him so long. Brendan said he was talking to Jesus. "In the tabernacle?" his father asked. "No," Brendan said, "in the light above the tabernacle." According to Brendan's confessor, the Church was entirely dark. There was no light above the tabernacle.

Are you prone to despair or to nostalgia for sweeter times? Do you long for a time of great saints and spiritual giants? Consider that we have lived when this holy boy lived. I implore you: do not miss the time in which God has placed you.

Consider a little girl whose picture sits on the desk of Supreme Court justice Clarence Thomas. It is held together by a frame of Popsicle sticks that she made. Why would such a powerful man give her image such a place of prominence? Because he knew her, and he knew she was a saint.

Margaret Leo was born with spina bifida, a dangerous curving of the spine. She spent her life in a wheelchair, all bent over and always grinning ear to ear. She bore her pain and suffering with joyful aplomb. At one point, doctors put titanium rods next to her spine to keep it from bending. Her spine bent the rods. What's more, one rod came poking out her back. She never complained.

To this day, her father, Leonard Leo, one of the most influential men in Washington, D.C., keeps those rods on his desk to remind him of what a really bad day can be. Parishioners at St. Thomas More Cathedral in Arlington, Virginia, remember fondly Margaret's simple faith. After receiving Communion, she would loudly exclaim, "Thank You, Jesus, for coming to me in the Blessed Sacrament." She would say this loudly and reverently, and people still say it in that cathedral at the morning Mass that Margaret attended.

At one summer softball game, Margaret fell into conversation with the father of a man named Edward Whelan, another highly influential man in Washington, D.C., legal circles. Whelan's father came away from the conversation saying, "I just met a living saint." When Margaret died not long after, her family began to find medals of St. Margaret Mary in unexpected places: on airplane seats, on the floor of a vacation cabin out west, in bowls of candies in hotel rooms. The family is certain that these were messages from Heaven and that their own little Margaret was perfectly well and in the Beatific Vision. Then came a miracle.

Ed Whelan's father collapsed. He was thought to have a deadly brain tumor and not long to live. The Leo family and the Whelan family began praying to the saint that Whelan's father had met only weeks before on that softball field. Within a week, Whelan's father was cured. He played golf a few days later. The little grinning girl, hunched over in her wheelchair, had struck again for Heaven. (When I first wrote about her story in a column at The Catholic Thing website, we were inundated with requests for her prayer card from all over the world.)

Another little suffering soul was Audrey Stevenson, who lived in a suburb of Paris. She was a little girl who brought an intense Catholic faith into her lukewarm family. At three years old, she crafted little yellow crosses with which she decorated each room in their Parisian apartment. She set up a prayer altar, where she would sit and pray to the Blessed Mother. Her mother says one day when little Audrey finished with her prayer, she stood up and exclaimed, "There, I've comforted her" and scampered off to play.

As Audrey walked home from school one day, her mother noticed that she was limping and asked her why. She discovered that Audrey had stuck pencils in her shoes. She told her mother, "*Je résiste.*" ("I resist.") She was teaching herself mortification. No one had taught her this. Somehow she seemed to have discerned the spiritual practice all on her own. Her parents were so alarmed by her spiritual precocity they went to the local parish priest and told him they did not know where she was learning all these things. His advice? "Follow her." So they did. It became especially difficult, however, when she was diagnosed with leukemia just a few years later.

Her mother advised her that they would follow everything the doctors wanted her to do and that things would therefore be all right. Five-year-old Audrey, barely catechized, corrected her mother: "No, Mummy, we will do what Jesus said. We will live like the birds in the trees." Her parents did not know where she had learned this. But this was the direction in which she took her whole family.

Thus began two years of intense, painful treatment. In addition to her physical pain, the essential immodesty of medical treatment also upset her. She did not like to see the flirting that went on among the doctors and nurses. But she persevered. When she received her bone marrow transplant, generally a last longshot when it comes to cancer treatment, she could be heard in her sterile hospital room singing songs to Mary.

Under Siege

During her two years of suffering, rosary groups sprang up all over France. Grown men prayed the prayer they had not prayed since they were little. Once her aunt was visiting Lyon in the South of France, and she stopped in at a church to pray. A woman in the church offered her a prayer card for "a little girl suffering from leukemia in Paris." She looked at the card, then looked into the woman's eyes, and said, "That is my niece."

Audrey had a special dedication to priestly vocations. She prayed for vocations intensely, especially for her uncle who drifted in and out of seminaries, unable to ground his life. Toward the end, as she lay dying, she asked for her uncle and was told that he had gone to Rome to enter yet another seminary. She said, "Good. Now I can rest." Those were nearly her final words on Earth.

Subsequently, her cult has grown. The Carmelite nuns at El Escorial, the palace of the kings of Spain outside Madrid, requested her Confirmation dress. Today it hangs in their chapter house.

Much of her family became engaged in the Church. Several of her brothers and sisters joined religious congregations, and her parents' apartment in Paris became a way station for Catholics entering apostolic life in Europe. One of their guests was a young man from Mexico. He told Audrey's father that, years before, he had contemplated suicide because he had cancer, but that he had found comfort and strength in the story of a little girl in Paris with cancer who was praying for religious vocations. Audrey's father, Jerome, replied with tears in his eyes, "You are sitting in her room."

We lived when this little saint lived. Embrace this most remarkable age.

We live in a world that avoids suffering and runs headlong from pain. We spend hundreds of billions of dollars to dull even the smallest pain. But remember that Jesus turned down the sponge soaked in pain reliever; and only the Catholic Church teaches that pain is blessed because it is a tool that God uses to sanctify us. Somehow these children knew that, and they allowed their pain to help redeem the world.

Notice also that none of these children were shepherds living in remote regions and tilling the soil. They lived among great affluence and great power. Margaret and Brendan lived in Northern Virginia, among the richest zip codes in the world. Margaret's father, Leonard Leo, consults with presidents and is one of the architects of the Trump administration's Supreme Court. Brendan Kelly's father, Frank, is the head of global government relations for Deutsche Bank, one of the largest financial institutions in the world. He is close friends with top government officials all over the world. Audrey Stevenson comes from old Chicago banking money. She lived in Paris—but they all lived in spiritual deserts crowded with the mirages of money and influence and power. Yet it was there that they were each called by Christ and heard His message of what it is to be human. God knows what He is about.

Amazingly, children like these have even revealed a truth to the Church herself. Until recently, the Church did not accept the idea that children could fully live all the virtues and therefore minor children could be raised to the altars only as martyrs, such as those from the early Church. Benedict XVI changed this and opened the door for nonmartyred children to be canonized. The children of Fatima, who suffered harrowing pain, were the first to be recognized as saints. Many believe mistakenly that they were saints because the Blessed Mother appeared to them. But, in fact, they are saints because of all that they endured for the Faith by carrying the message of Fatima;

and they are saints for suffering the Spanish flu and offering their suffering for others.

Many other children have suffered greatly, died young, and brought the Faith to others. Little Nellie of Holy God (1903–1908), a five-year-old who lived with nuns in Ireland, begged to receive the Eucharist before the age at which it was then allowed. In 1910, Pope St. Pius X changed the age for Eucharistic reception based on the case of Little Nellie of Holy God. You should find and read her story.

Flannery O'Connor wrote about Mary Ann Long (1946–1959), a little girl with a deadly malady who was given into the care of a convent of nuns in Atlanta by her family. Mary Ann Long did not die as expected but became a profoundly holy child known throughout the Catholic community in Atlanta. Her story is repeated to this day.

A Roman girl, Antonietta Meo (1930–1937), lost a leg from cancer. She said it was a gift to Jesus. She wrote love letters to Jesus that came to the attention of Pope Pius XI, who made her story widely known. In 2007, Pope Benedict XVI declared her "Venerable." You can venerate her relics at the Basilica of Santa Croce in Rome.

Fifteen-year-old Carlo Acutis (1991–2006) has been beatified. He was discovered to be incorrupt.

Contemplate this fact: you have lived in a time of very great saints and spiritual giants.

Great Debates

The lives of all these children also turn our minds to one of the greatest debates of all time, one in which we are privileged to be able to participate: the debate over the nature of the human person. I want to emphasize this: we are living through one of the greatest debates the Church has ever known. We are privileged to live during this debate.

At important times throughout history, the Church has been called upon to decide fundamental questions. The early Church had to answer certain questions about the nature of Jesus Christ. The Arians argued the Jesus was brought into being through the Father's will, and therefore He had a beginning and therefore He was not of the same essence as the Father. But as the Church prayed for understanding about the Trinity, it was eventually decided that the Father and Son are indeed of the same substance, and this was expressed in the Nicene Creed, though the debate continued to rage.

The early Church also wrestled with questions about the nature of the Church. In the Acts of the Apostles, the question of whether Gentiles could be members of the Church was considered, as was the question of who would rule, a council of presbyters or a single bishop. And there was the ongoing question of the authority of the bishop of Rome. These debates about the Church continued through the Middle Ages, particularly around the investiture crisis and the rise of the Protestant Reformers. Luther believed the Church had "lost sight of the doctrine of grace" and had "lost its claim to be considered the authentic Christian Church." The Catholic Church claimed then, as it does now, to be the only Church founded by Christ, maintaining that all other institutions that describe themselves as churches are really ecclesial communities founded by men. The Catholic Church alone was, and is, infallible and indefectible. Though these debates were never settled, at least they eventually settled down.

As harrowing as these debates were at the time, those who lived through them were honored by God to have been placed in the very times in which these important truths were considered. By His own providence, God allowed these debates to arise and with them the heresies that allowed us to sharpen our understanding and beliefs. Although such debates were profoundly unsettling and roiled the ancient world, we look back upon those times with great envy. Why? Because those times were so vital to the life of the Church and the world. Oh, to have been present at such times!

Yet we are. We have now come to the present age, when the nature of man himself is up for debate. And we have been asked to participate. This is one of the greatest debates in the history of the world. Is someone with Down syndrome fully human? Is it possible to create a fully human person using the DNA of an animal? Is it possible for a woman to marry another woman? Is it licit to create a human being in a test tube? Is an unborn child no more than a clump of insensate cells that we may destroy or nurture according to our whim? Is the unborn child a person? Or is she property? Can a boy be a girl? Or a girl become a boy? Is homosexuality a new category of being unto itself? Are there fifty-seven genders? These are all questions about the nature of man.

The psalmist asks, "What is man that thou art mindful of him?" (8:4). And what else is the rise of identity politics except a search for Who Am I? Mankind has become profoundly unsettled. And rather than become unsettled by living in these times, the proper response must be gratitude that God has sent us here and now to help answer these questions.

It may seem at this moment that we are losing these debates. But there was a time when most of the Christian world was Arian, including most bishops. In fact, even though that question was eventually settled by the Church, there are still many Arians around the world. They just go by other names. Our friends the

Latter-day Saints are Arian. The Muslims are Arians too. Many Christians are Arian. Even the debate about the nature of the Church continues: Protestant sects are still multiplying, and even many Catholics come to question the claims the Church makes about herself.

And what of the human person? At this moment, a majority of people would argue that abortion at some stage in development may be regrettable but morally permissible. A vast majority would consider the buying and selling of human eggs for surrogate gestation to be not only permissible but a blessing. Many believe homosexuals are created as homosexual by God at conception and that homosexuals are therefore a different category of being. Many are uncomfortable thinking about human-animal chimera; but if it works to our benefit, many think it is probably fine and good. Most people now believe it is acceptable to create and harvest human ova in order to create vaccines. The buying and selling of aborted baby parts is acceptable to many.

Some look at this and react in fear. Others retreat into distraction and nostalgia. But looking even at all this, I say: never has there been a finer time to be a faithful Catholic. We are living through a global debate as significant as all the other great debates that have taken hold of the world. Live not in fear.

The Church Is Dying

How could this be a good time to be a faithful Catholic when the Church is dying? Church attendance is down. Priestly vocations are down. Convents emptied out starting sixty years ago. Catholic writer Glenn Stanton provides an interesting look behind these sorts of statistics. In his book *The Myth of the Dying Church*, Stanton looks primarily at the Protestant and Evangelical churches. He finds the assertion of a dying Church to be true but only for those denominations that have followed the State Church. Mainline Protestant churches have given in to the State Church on most questions, starting with the Anglican surrender to contraception almost one hundred years ago. Along each step of the way toward what they think is "progress," they have lost more and more of their congregations. When a church downplays gospel truths and professes nothing but the modern zeitgeist, a person has to wonder why he ought to stay. According to a research study carried out by Indiana University and Harvard, mainline Protestants declined from 35 percent of the American population in 1972 to no more than 12 percent in 2016. Stanton says this happened as these communities began to doubt "the existence of miracles, the reality of sin, and the actual atoning death of Christ and His resurrection, as well as jettisoning biblical convictions about sex, gender issues and abortion."[103]

Data shows these folks are leaving the mainline churches and joining the ranks of the nones. Research also shows that these nones may never have believed central truths all along or at best were raised in lukewarm households, neither hot nor cold. I remember a friend of mine who left Christian practice as a young man, saying, "We stopped going to Church when we discovered fly-fishing." And as I explored earlier, these nones really do not believe in nothing. Like all of us, they hunger for truth and are careening about in myriad and often crazy ways to find it.

---

[103] Glenn T. Stanton, "No, Christianity Doesn't Need to Endorse Homosexuality to Grow," *Federalist*, May 6, 2019, https://the-federalist.com/2019/05/06/no-christianity-doesnt-need-endorse-homosexuality-grow/.

What we see in Protestant circles is an emptying out of the mainline churches but at the same time a continuing and often explosive growth in the Evangelical, Fundamentalist, and Pentecostal sects. According to the Indiana-Harvard study, such churches grew from 39 percent of church attendees in 1989 to 47 percent in 2017. These are the sects delivering the pure, Bible-based Protestant faith. Glenn Stanton tells the story of a Bible-based Eastlake Church in Seattle that grew by leaps and bounds under the "hipster" guidance of Pastor Ryan Meeks. More than a hundred new people were showing up each week. But then, a few years ago, Meeks joined the zeitgeist. He caved in to the LGBTs. More than merely welcoming them, he decided his church would affirm them. He said, "I don't care if the Bible says, 'Gay people suck.' I have lots of things I disagree with about the Bible." Meeks's megachurch imploded practically overnight. Congregants ran for the exits. Meeks's budget cratered. Employees were let go, including the lesbian he changed everything for.

That, in a nutshell, tells the story of religiosity in America. It is bad news for those who want to trim theological sails but good news for those who want their sails filled with gospel truth. One of the remarkable points in Stanton's book is that Americans are more religious in our era than at any time in American history. The impression we have of our founding generation as deeply religious is not entirely true: in colonial times, no more than 17 percent of the population went to church regularly.

What about Catholicism? That is a harder one to analyze for the reason supposedly given by James Joyce about the Church: "Here comes everybody." As Stanton, who is a convert from Evangelicalism to Catholicism, explains, we are all thrown together. Left, right, and center each call themselves Catholic. Those who question the teaching on contraception are in the same churches as those who accept it all. Without a doubt, attendance is down, vocations are down, and polls show that increasing numbers no longer believe the teachings of the Church. There is often an uncertain trumpet from our bishops, and even from the Vatican. There has been the priest sex scandal and the poor showing of the bishops in dealing with it. Social-science data shows it is mostly Catholics who are heading into the none category.

This may sound shocking, but this winnowing is not necessarily a bad thing. Many of those leaving the Church were not true believers anyway but a kind of fifth column inside the Church. They may have called themselves Catholic, but many were dissenters who mostly contributed to the confusion. I have written about a woman named Melinda Selmys, a self-described "queer" living in a mixed marriage (her husband is not "queer") who has raised many children. As she left the Church, ironically under the Francis pontificate, which was supposed to stem the receding liberal tide of those like Selmys, she announced she had never believed in the central teachings of the Church. Yet, for years, she had been allowed a platform in the Church to air her "questions." She was even published by orthodox presses such as Our Sunday Visitor. I wrote that it was a good thing that she left the Church. Better to take your dissent elsewhere.

Another person I have written about is the columnist Damon Linker, who interned under Fr. Richard Neuhaus at *First Things* and then paid him back with a vicious book-length attack. As Linker announced his exit from the Church, he, too, noted that he had never believed in certain foundational teachings. I saluted their honest apostasy. Others, like Fr. James Martin, who is heretical on the question of human sexuality, ought to have the honesty to leave the Church. But he won't. He knows what happened to Charles Curran, a dissenter on contraception, who is no longer allowed to teach Catholic theology. When he decamped to Southern Methodist University, many stopped listening to him. This is why so many dissenters prefer to stay in the Church; it is how they gain and maintain an audience. The Church is their platform to spread their confusion.

This is the Catholic version of what Stanton described happening among mainline Protestants. Yes, vocations are down overall, but they are up at places such as the Priestly Fraternity of Saint Peter, which promotes the Traditional Latin Mass. Vocations are way up at the Institute of Christ the King Sovereign Priest. They are up in orthodox dioceses and among congregations of orthodox nuns.

Consider that in June 2020, the Archdiocese of New York ordained just two priests, only one of whom was for the archdiocese itself. Cardinal Dolan has a reputation for orthodoxy, but his archdiocese doesn't. This is a diocese that allows homosexual parishes to run wild in New York City. The archbishop himself may hold fast to the teachings of the Church, but he has allowed Church groups to march in the deeply sinful annual homosexual parade. Cardinal Dolan may be a strong advocate for orthodoxy, but he permits out-and-proud gay churches to flourish, such as St. Paul the Apostle (called St. Paul the Apostate by some) on Manhattan's West Side, St. Francis of Assisi in Midtown, and the Jesuit Church of St. Francis Xavier. Even St. Patrick's Cathedral is on Yelp's list of "gay-friendly" parishes in New York City. Good heavens!

At the time of what Fr. Neuhaus called the "Long Lent" in 2002, when the priest sex scandals first broke into the open, Fr. Benedict Groeschel said that young men would respond to their Mother Church coming under attack. They would move to defend her. They would offer up their lives to defend her. He said the numbers of good seminarians would grow. Understand that he said this as it became widely known that predatory homosexuals had run wild in American parishes and that, to a large extent, the bishops had behaved abominably, moving the abusers around, treating victims and their families badly, and hiding the situation from the larger Church and the world. When you think about it, of course we should expect young men to come hurrying to the aid of their Mother.

Certainly vocations are far below what they were at midcentury, when vocations vanished and Mass attendance dropped seemingly overnight. But they have increased from twenty years ago, even after several decades of incessant slander against the Church and priests and bishops, some of it very well deserved. You would think that after the sex scandal 1.0, the sex scandal 2.0, the McCarrick affair, and much else, young men would stay far away from the Church, even if they thought God was calling them. Not so. More young men are coming. And these young seminarians are rock solid. Writing at *First Things* in the summer of 2019, papal biographer George Weigel said that the seminarians he has met are "impressive, intellectually alert and engaged; deeply pious without being cloyingly sentimental; able to interact with (and offer a real witness to) fellow students in a multinational context of Catholic men and women; and much more mature than I remember seminarians being four decades ago."[104]

More and better seminarians are not the whole story either. There are also the young and habited nuns. Have you seen the

[104] George Weigel, "In Praise of Today's Seminarians," *First Things* (August 28, 2019), https://www.firstthings.com/web-exclusives /2019/08/in-praise-of-todays-seminarians.

direct-mail package from the Ann Arbor Dominicans? The cover line is "We are experiencing a different kind of vocations crisis." Their postulancy is bursting at the seams. They do not have enough room for all who want to come. And they are not the only ones. The Norbertines in California are having the same problem, as are many other congregations of nuns that both adhere to the teachings of the Church and wear the habit. A Jewish writer named Eve Fairbanks wrote a lengthy piece in the left-wing *Huffington Post* about young and very accomplished women who are hungering to answer God's call to the religious life.[105] In 2017, 13 percent of women ages eighteen to thirty-five who answered a Georgetown survey said they had considered becoming a religious sister. Fairbanks points out that that is roughly nine hundred thousand women. On the website VocationMatch.com, you can answer a dozen questions and be matched with the religious vocation that would be right for you. In years past, this website would get a few hundred queries. In 2018, they received 2,600, and most of the requests were for fully habited orders.

Fairbanks tells the story of a Catholic school in Maryland called St. Mary's Ryken that invited religious brothers and sisters into one of the classes to talk about the religious life. These talks were rather insipid, and the students demonstrated an utter lack of interest. One priest showed a video of a priest dancing to the song "Greased Lightning" in a chorus line of teenage boys. The priest asked, "Do priests dance? Yes, we do. We're just like you."[106] Appalling, right? Consider the kind of school that would allow

---

[105] Eve Fairbanks, "Behold, the Millennial Nuns," *Huffington Post*, July 11, 2019, https://www.huffpost.com/highline/article/millennial-nuns/.
[106] Ibid.

this kind of presentation — certainly not one that cares about souls. The school's mission-and-values page does not mention Christ even a single time. But it mentions the great god "diversity" three times.

Fairbanks reports that "a couple of years ago, a sterner priest came to talk." The priest dressed all in black with "a tight clerical collar." He told the students that they were "called to holiness," that they were "called to be saints." The teacher sat at his desk wincing and thinking this straight-no-chaser presentation of the Faith would not appeal to his students. This is the typical belief many adults have about young people, though it is quite the opposite of the admonition St. John Paul II gave never to settle for mediocrity; and quite the opposite of Fr. Neuhaus's call to live the high adventure of Catholic orthodoxy. When a lacrosse player asked the teacher if the priest was coming back, the teacher's response was "Oh no, don't worry." But the kid said, "I want him back."[107] Oldsters think kids want hipness and fun, even goofiness. But they don't. They want the real stuff, the straight stuff, the hard stuff. They want to be challenged. They want to be saints.

There are those who understand this, and they come from unlikely places. For example, Attorney General William Barr delivered a speech at Notre Dame in 2020 that riled his opponents mightily. They accused him of calling for a theocratic state. What did he say? "Social order must flow up from the people themselves, freely obeying the dictates of inwardly possessed and commonly shared moral values.... They must flow from a transcendent Supreme Being." Barr assessed the enemy accurately: "Modern secularists dismiss this idea of morality as otherworldly superstition imposed by a kill-joy clergy." Ominously, Barr warned that

[107] Ibid.

the moral pendulum we expect to swing back from this lawlessness may not swing back at all. He describes a pervasive force, fervor, and comprehensive assault on religion that is not decay but destruction.[108]

This is strong stuff from the attorney general. But nowhere in this speech do you hear despair. He does warn against distraction: "The pervasiveness and power of our high-tech popular culture fuels apostasy in another way. It provides an unprecedented degree of distraction."[109] Dreher says we must strategically retreat. Barr says, charge! As Napoleon said, "Boldness, boldness, always boldness."

Writing four years ago, Msgr. Charles Pope of Washington, D.C., said something similar. "It is zero dark thirty in our post-Christian culture," and it is time for Catholics to go to war. He said, "There is a growing consternation among some Catholics that the Church, at least in her leadership, is living in the past. It seems there is no awareness that we are at war and that Catholics need to be summoned." His call is not to despair or to nostalgia or to distraction but to action. "Simply put, it is time for clergy to prepare themselves and God's people for sacrifice. Seeking to compromise with this culture is now unthinkable. Our only recourse is to seek to lance the boil."[110]

---

[108] Attorney General William P. Barr's remarks to the Law School and the de Nicola Center for Ethics and Culture at the University of Notre Dame, South Bend, Indiana, October 11, 2019, https://www.justice.gov/opa/speech/attorney-general-william-p-barr-delivers-remarks-law-school-and-de-nicola-center-ethics.

[109] Ibid.

[110] Msgr. Charles Pope, "Comfort Catholicism Has to Go; It Is Time to Prepare for Persecution," *National Catholic Register*, August 21, 2016, https://www.ncregister.com/blog/comfort-catholicism-has-to-go-it-is-time-to-prepare-for-persecution.

Under Siege

The great Cardinal George of Chicago recognized that it takes no courage to conform to government and social pressure. On the other hand, he said, "swimming against the tide means limiting one's access to positions of prestige and power in society. It means that those who choose to live by the Catholic faith will not be welcomed as political candidates for national office, will not sit on editorial boards of major newspapers, will not be at home on most university faculties, will not have successful careers as actors and entertainers. Nor will their children who will also be suspect."[111] But there is no despair here, no nostalgia, no distraction.

Professor Robert George of Princeton made similar calls to action at the National Catholic Prayer Breakfast and the annual dinner for the Washington, D.C.–based Catholic Information Center. Like Professor Steven D. Smith of the University of San Diego, George sees the utter destruction all around us as well as the rise of new paganism. Yet he vociferously argues against compromise, accommodation, or strategic retreat. "I don't see what we should be retreating from, even strategically. And to what, or where, could we retreat? To our families, religious communities, civil society associations? They'll hunt us down and dismantle our institutions."[112] Professor George even uses the word *despair* to characterize the feelings many Christian parents have of being

---

[111] Quoted in "Catholics in America Will—and Do—Suffer for 'Swimming against the Tide,'" Catholic News Agency, September 12, 2014, https://www.catholicnewsagency.com/news/catholics-in-america-will---and-do---suffer-for-swimming-against-the-tide-89185.

[112] Robert George, Remarks at the 2019 Catholic Information Center Annual Dinner, October 23, 2019, https://mirrorofjustice.blogs.com/mirrorofjustice/2019/10/remarks-at-the-2019-catholic-information-center-annual-dinner.html.

able to protect their children. Many believe we have entered a new Diocletian age. But we have no choice but to fight. And there are many ways to fight, some of which I will consider in the epilogue. But make no mistake: the only other option is to surrender.

In June 1944, as the landing craft hit Utah Beach and the ramps crashed into the waves, it is likely that every boy and man plunging into the battle experienced a jumble of thoughts and emotions. First, the abject terror that an incoming shell might take off his head. Second, a great regret that he had to do this terrible thing, whatever consequences he might suffer. But a third emotion, softer but powerful enough in the end to spur him onward, was the great sense of honor that he was called to do it, to fight for his country, for his family and friends, for Western civilization against the pagan Nazis. Don't forget, even Jesus Christ wished to forgo the terrible cup of suffering He foresaw being offered to Him. This is very natural, very human. But then He went forward, as did those boys and men at Normandy. We are on that beach now, you and I and everyone you know who bears the mark of Baptism on our souls; we are in the Garden of Gethsemane. We may pray for deliverance. But we must go forward, no matter the cost.

If we must battle our enemies on the social, political, and cultural heights, if we must fight all those in the news media, academia, Hollywood, billionaire foundations, government, the official state religion, in short, all those who hate us, we should also remember and be glad that they are, all of them, obsessed with us.

Catholics are doing good and noble work. There is not another religion on the planet that so captivates the attention of these elites. Does anyone on the planet worry or even think about what the head of the Episcopal Church says or thinks about anything? Does anyone who is not a Methodist even know who heads the Methodist church or any other "mainline" faith? Yet the elite hang on every word of the bishop of Rome. Every utterance the pope makes on an airplane makes global news. Remember when the family synod considered a nuanced change in the Church's description of homosexuality? It made front-page news all over the globe. As the 1960s comedian Lenny Bruce said, "There is only one 'The Church'."

And if we look at recent Church history, we see things that any age of the Church will look upon with envy. Consider the Second Vatican Council, a meeting of the bishops that captivated the world and even today continues to roil global debates. Remember Paul VI's encyclical on contraception, how it flew in the face of all "enlightened" opinion and captured the attention of the whole world? Recall Pope Paul's death and the rise of the man from Poland, who, from the moment he boomed, "Be not afraid" from the balcony of St. Peter's Basilica, required the world's attention.

I want to draw your attention to a handful of events that happened one after another. They each singly and all together demonstrate what a remarkable time we are living in and show how the world is obsessed with the Catholic Church.

It starts with our great shame in 2002, when the story broke of widespread sexual abuse of young men at the hands of sexually aberrant priests. Even in our shame, our public and painful suffering related to sexually aberrant priests, the whole world watched. Would they have watched any other quite so closely? Notice how hard the homophiles tried to insist that it had nothing to do with homosexuality; that it was "only" about pedophilia or the obscure ephebophilia, a sexual attraction to adolescents. The ongoing fight about the nature of the priest sex scandal is just one small measure of how the world obsesses about the Catholic Church.

Because of the homosexual priest scandal, the Church is on fire. Yet still, brave and good young men are running into the burning building to become holy priests. Their courage is reminiscent of a picture I am looking at, a picture of young Marines, stationed at Marine headquarters in Washington, D.C., running full tilt into a burning high-rise home for the elderly. These are the same sort of young men who are running to the priesthood, even in these dark days. As Fr. Groeschel predicted, young men have responded because their Mother is under attack.

But, even as the sex abuse tragedy unfolded, do you remember what happened next? In the very shadow of the Long Lent, Mel Gibson released *The Passion of the Christ*. Never forget what a global event that was.

Genius that he is, Gibson released *The Passion* on Ash Wednesday, February 25, 2004. I was in a New York hotel room on the day it was released. Every single television network was talking about it. Every single talking head was talking about it—and not just the movie but the actual Passion of Our Lord. True, this was a broadly Christian event. But let's be blunt: it was a uniquely Catholic vision. It was the Sorrowful Mysteries of the Rosary; it was the Stations of the Cross. *The Passion of the Christ* showed the supernatural relationship between Our Lord and Our Mother Mary; His eyes were on her, and Satan's eyes were on Him.

Grossing $370 million domestically, *The Passion* was the number-one movie in America for three weeks running. Globally, it grossed $622 million. Can you believe that a realistic, bloody movie about the torture of Christ did all this? Do you remember seeing it? Do you remember the hushed and weeping audience?

In January 2004, Dan Leach strangled his girlfriend Ashley Nicole because he did not want the baby she was carrying. He forged a note that made it look as if she had committed suicide. The local medical examiner ruled the death a suicide. A month later, *The Passion of the Christ* came to a small theater in Richmond, just outside Houston. Dan Leach went to see it. Shortly thereafter, he walked into the sheriff's office and confessed to killing Ashley. The sheriff said, "When he came in, he was very, very cooperative and gave us explicit details of how he had planned the murder, committed it, and the things he had done nobody else could have known because the information was not public knowledge. He had to have been there because he had knowledge of what had gone on during the murder." Dan Leach recounted, "I went and saw the movie with a couple friends. It was very intense, and having that visual stimuli really helps you to focus; it does move you. After watching that movie I was very emotional. I thought about the things I had done, and I was up-set that I hadn't repented yet."[113] Leach went first to his church and confessed, and then to the authorities. He is now serving a seventy-five-year sentence.

In March 2004, Turner Lee Bingham walked up to a group of cops and told them he had robbed a wireless store, where he had taken eighty dollars from the register. He told them *The Passion of the Christ* had inspired him to turn himself in.

James Anderson saw the movie, too. Afterward, he confessed to a three-year-old unsolved robbery. He had walked into the First Union Bank in Palm Beach, grabbed a female employee,

---

[113] "Texas Passion Case: Criminal Confesses after Viewing 'The Passion,'" excerpt from Jody Eldred, *Changed Lives: Miracles of the Passion* (New York: Good Times Entertainment, 2004), CBN, https://www.cbn.com/entertainment/screen/passion_el-dred_texaspassion.aspx?mobile=false&q=entertainment/screen/Passion_eldred_texaspassion.aspx&option=print.

and forced tellers to hand over twenty-five thousand dollars. He was scot-free. *The Passion* made him clear his conscience.

It wasn't just in the United States that this happened either. In Oslo, Norway, a month after the movie opened, Johnny Olsen walked into a newspaper office and confessed to two bombings of Blitz House, a headquarters for left-wing youth. He had bombed Blitz House ten years earlier. The police had suspected him of the bombing, but they were never able to connect him to the crime. His lawyer said the movie hit him like a "bolt of lightning."

Imagine the cops' reaction when they learned that these men were confessing because of a movie. Nobody confessed after seeing *Spiderman* or *Shrek 2*.

That was 2004. Do you remember what else happened in 2004? John Kerry, a dissenting Catholic, presented himself as a candidate for president of the United States. And what did we see? We witnessed a national, even international, debate about the duties of the Catholic voter. But more than that, we witnessed a debate about the proper reception of the Holy Eucharist! Do you remember that? Have we ever seen such a thing as that? If you google "John Kerry Communion," more than 2.7 million hits come up—and perhaps you'll find Cardinal Ratzinger's *Worthiness to Receive Communion: General Principles* from the Congregation for the Doctrine of the Faith. The future pope said the only way a Catholic could vote for a pro-abortion politician was for "proportionate" reasons, and, even then, the voter would be considered in "remote material cooperation" in great evil. This memo was so explosive that when it was sent to ex-cardinal Theodore McCarrick, he suppressed most of it. In fact, he lied to his brother bishops who were then meeting in Colorado, telling them the memo allowed for Communion to politicians who persist in their support for abortion, the opposite of what the memo actually said.[114] The scandal came to light only after the memo was leaked to an Italian publication.

Perhaps you'll find stories too about Archbishop Burke of Saint Louis or Archbishop Bruskewitz of Lincoln, Nebraska. Both said Kerry would be denied Communion if he presented himself in their dioceses. This was news all over the world. Even Cardinal Arinze of the Vatican said those like Kerry were "not fit" to receive the Body and Blood of Our Lord Jesus Christ.

The noted philanderer and woman-slaughterer Teddy Kennedy was furious. He ripped into Pope John Paul II. Kennedy complained that the pope had given Communion to Chilean strongman Augusto Pinochet, though this was false. So potent was this issue that it made the *New York Times* when Kerry was given the Eucharist at the Paulist Center in Boston on Easter. It is said Kerry attended the Paulist Center because it was one of the few places that would not hassle him.

I do not believe we have ever seen anything quite like this before in our history. But there was more. Even before we could catch our breath, what did we see? In 2005, we saw the beginning of the final suffering of our beloved Pope John Paul the Great.

Do you remember this?

Everyone in the world watched as the pope began to fade, hunched and crippled. We saw his face as it became a mask of pain. But we also noticed that he hardly slowed down. He may not have gathered crowds of millions anymore, but he was there among us, on the balcony, presiding over his Wednesday audiences and praying for us, always praying for us. I remember standing in

---

[114] "How McCarrick Pulled a Fast One on His Brother Bishops," *California Catholic Daily*, August 23, 2020, https://www.cal-catholic.com/how-mccarrick-pulled-a-fast-one-on-his-brother-bishops/.

St. Peter's Square in his final year, listening to him speak. His voice was no more than a croak. You could barely understand him. But he was there.

Then, in the waxing days of 2005, right after the presidential election that saw the Eucharist in our national debate, things began to take a dramatic turn. It was reported that the pope had the flu, which is why the Vatican canceled his public events on January 31. He was admitted to the Gemelli Polyclinic Hospital on the evening of February 2. This was the first time he had been hospitalized since an appendicitis operation in 1996. He was suffering from tracheitis, an inflammation of the windpipe, along with spasms of the larynx. Though the Vatican downplayed the problem, papal spokesman Ciro Benedettini said the pope was having trouble breathing. An American doctor said the complications were "ominous and unusual."[115]

The Holy Father returned to the Vatican eight days later, on February 10. Two weeks later, however, they rushed him back to Gemelli, where he underwent a tracheotomy. On March 13, he returned to the Vatican for the very last time. There is a picture of the Holy Father leaving Gemelli in a van, a huge crowd of medical personnel standing around it. I was in Rome that eerie, ominous night, with empty streets, a chill in the air, and the sky spitting. The whole world was there too, watching.

On March 27, Pope John Paul II came to his apartment window to bless the crowd that stood in St. Peter's Square, waiting and watching. He tried to read the words of the Apostolic Blessing but failed. It was Easter Sunday.

---

[115] "Ailing Pope in Hospital with Flu," *Chicago Tribune*, February 2, 2005, http://www.chicagotribune.com/news/ct-xpm-2005-02-02-0502020278-story.html.

After failing to speak on Easter Sunday, four days later, he suffered septic shock caused by a urinary tract infection and the collapse of his cardiocirculatory system. His temperature rose to 103. Mass was said at the foot of his bed.

Two days later, on April 2, another Mass was said in his presence. The Holy Father spoke his final words;[116] "Let me go to the house of the Father." He slipped into a coma, and two hours later he was gone.

Thousands were under his window. People were crowded in St. Peter's Square, shoulder to shoulder, weeping, saying their beads. The front of St. Peter's was lit up. The lights in the pope's apartment were still blazing when a bevy of bishops stood on the balcony and made the announcement. Oddly, the crowd began to clap. Perhaps not so odd, for they knew he had gone to his great reward after years of suffering, years of teaching us how to suffer and then how to die.

Do you remember where you were when you heard the news? I was at the Longlea retreat house outside Culpepper in rural Virginia. We had gathered around my car, all the doors open, the radio on, listening to the news, waiting for the news.

The crowd in St. Peter's sang a Salve, and then the huge bell began to toll. People all over the world dropped to their knees and prayed. People of all faiths raised their voices in praise and prayer for this good and great man. This was a global event. The whole world watched.

And do you remember how they kept watching through the following dramatic days? Do you recall how Rome began to fill

---

[116] "Vatican Reveals Pope John Paul II's Last Words: 'Let Me Go to the House of the Father,'" Catholic News Agency, September 19, 2005, https://www.catholicnewsagency.com/news/vatican_reveals_pope_john_paul_ii_lasts_words_let_me_go_to_the_house_of_the_father.

up with pilgrims? First, they came from around Italy; then from other points in Europe and the United States; then from the Philippines and from all over the world. Millions dropped whatever they were doing and went to Rome. Many had no place to sleep and no plan but to thank Our Holy Father. So they slept on the streets, waiting to file past his coffin and to participate in his funeral. Do you remember those images? Do you remember the book of the Gospel laying open on his casket, the pages ruffling in the wind?

After John Paul the Great's final suffering, death, and burial, the whole world kept watching, anxious to see who the next pope would be. Did you notice that even our Evangelical friends felt they had a stake in the new pope? When the white smoke rose and the bells rang, a few hundred thousand ran to the square, and hundreds of millions ran to their television sets to hear the ancient call, "*Habemus papam!*" We have a pope! I don't believe that the whole world has ever watched so intently, and for so long, our Holy Mother Church.

Within a few years of that blessed event, we had a national debate over health care. You may not remember, but we saw the Church's teaching on abortion in the middle of the debate. We saw the Church stand toe to toe with the powers of the earth and demand that abortion not be a part of Obamacare. The entire bill was held up because of these concerns of the Church.

Then almost before we knew it, Pope Benedict resigned, and the news shook not just our Catholic world but the world over. The election of another pope soon followed, and his every controversial utterance lands on the front page of newspapers around the globe.

And so, I say again, in the history of the world, we have never seen a time like this, when the whole world watched so intently, and for so long, our Holy Catholic Church. We are living in one of the most remarkable epochs the Church has ever seen. I implore you not to miss it.

God the Father knows what He is about. He knows, He knew, what a horrific epoch this would be. He knew from the founding of the world. He knew everything would be under attack. He knew about abortion, pornography, divorce, drugs. He knew about homosexuals coming to attack our Church from inside and out. And whom did He send? You. And me. How appalling and how wonderful is that! He sent us right here and right now. You cannot miss this moment. You cannot miss your mission. It is yours alone. Do not pass your time in fear, or nostalgia, or distraction. Embrace your time. For opportunities to do His will, we live in the most target-rich environment the world has ever known. As I keep telling you, there are halos hanging from the lowest branches of the trees. Reach up and grab one.

John Paul the Great said this new century would be a great Christian century, a great springtime of the faith hinting at glorious seasons to come. You and I may not live long enough to see the full flowering of this great age. We may live in one of those odd times, between ages, on the cusp of something new and wonderful. But when future Catholics look back upon us, they will look back with envy. We need not be envious of times past; we are already in the future's past, and our descendants will long to have been here with us, right here, right now, in these trying times, in places where troubles closed in all around us, when there were so few of us to fight back, times of great danger, times of great saints and spiritual giants, times where each faithful Catholic, each one of us, was so badly needed.

There is no finer time to be a faithful Catholic than right now.

Epilogue

Answering the Age-Old
Question of What to Do

What to do? What to do? That is the question I get the most when I travel around giving talks. And it is likely the question you have right now. What are we supposed to do?

Start the easy way. Stop saying "chair."

Unless you're talking about a place to sit down, stop saying "chair." Whoever is running a meeting is the chairman. You're entitled to some slack if you say "chairwoman." Never say, "chairperson." Ever. But starting right now, never say "chair."

It may seem like a small thing. After all, saying "chair" instead of "chairman" does not seem so important. But it is really quite huge. It is the tiny way they begin to bend our minds and our wills to them. Even on little things, we must resist. Circle behind them, go back to the beginning when they started this nonsense. They counted on us not to notice what they were doing. It will shock them that we are going back to square one.

While you're at it, say "Indian," even "American Indian," instead of "Native American." You'll get politically correct correction aplenty. Laugh it off. Given the Garden of Eden, no one is "native" or "indigenous" to this land. Again, it sounds like a little thing, but it means a great deal to the Left's ideologues. So, take it away from them. Let them know you won't play their silly games.

Never ever say "people of color." It is purely racist because it includes everyone except whites. That's their intention. Don't even say "African American." I recall with amusement a Canadian sportscaster during the Olympics who referred to a black athlete from Canada as an "African American." He did it over and over. What do you call a black German? What do you call a white South African? All these were intended to confuse you, even to control you. As I recall, late columnist Stanley Crouch referred to himself as "Negro." He said it had more dignity.

Above all, do not use their preferred "pronouns." Forcing someone to call a man "she" or "ze" or whatever craziness they insist upon is forcing that person to deny God's creation and even God Himself. Personal pronouns can only be "he" or "she" and this adheres only to those who are in fact "he" or "she." And do not buy into this utter fantasy world of cisgender and transgender. There are no such things. If they try to convince you otherwise, just keep saying, "There are no such things." Do not get lost in the thicket of their reasoning, such as it is.

I would go even further and suggest never to say "gender" unless you are talking about language. Always say "sex." Gender was made up by a child molester named Dr. John Money, who ran the Johns Hopkins "sex-change" clinic in Baltimore. He abused a boy under his care who was raised as a girl and who later committed suicide. Don't use "gender" ever.

Notice each of these examples comes from the leftist holy trinity of race, sex, and "gender." They want to lead us ideologically around by the nose. And they do this by messing with the language and forcing us to go along. Don't do it. Do not give in to political correctness. It is a kind of terrorism.

I am not recommending you do all this at work or on social media, especially if it can get you into serious trouble. But consider that there are three levels of fighting back. I will use local examples. After all, most of us are called to interact locally rather than nationally or internationally.

The three steps are "quiet and privately," "flying the flag," and "charging the sniper's nest."

First, act quietly and privately.

I told the anecdote from a war movie about soldiers who charge the sniper's nest. I suggest that we charge the sniper's nest, but I want to clarify that not everyone is called to that kind of work. In the culture wars, jobs can be lost; so can friends and even family members. So, many people will want to keep their powder dry. This does not mean you cannot help. You can.

Consider the men charging the sniper's nest. They could not do this without guns, ammo, uniforms, medicine, food. This is called the supply chain. Napoleon said an army marches on its stomach. That is the supply chain. In the culture wars, you can be a part of the supply chain. Give your time or treasure.

This can be quiet and private. Here's how.

Find a local group lobbying the school board, trying to get pornographic sex ed out of the school. Send them a check. Show up at a meeting and wish them well. Even something so small means a lot. That means a great deal to them because those who are charging the sniper's nest often feel alone. Above all, when they have a tough vote, show up and just sit there! They will know you're there. This does not mean you have to raise your head above the fox hole, make a speech, and maybe harm your career. Make these thanks private, quiet. That is fine.

Do you want to fight porn? Find a porn-fighting group and help them. I mentioned a nasty yet massive website called

PornHub. Find out who is fighting them. Send them a check every month!

Do you want to fight for the unborn child? Find the local group that prays in front of an abortion clinic. Join them. Is that your thing? Volunteer your time at their office. Send them a check.

Did I say send them a check? Let me tell you this. Every single group that is charging the sniper's nest has very little money. They get by on the widow's mite. Next to prayer, cash is the mother's milk of the culture wars. Our enemies literally have billions. We have next to nothing. Find a group and give. Find two groups and give. Put them in your will.

Second, fly the flag.

Flying the flag can be quite straightforward. Speak up. How many times have we simply swallowed our views for unity and comity, when all the while our left-wing friends let their flags fly?

Let your friends and family know your views.

During campaign season, put a sign in your yard. Put a bumper sticker on your car. Refuse to use the Left's linguistic tricks. Let people know that it is acceptable to disagree with those who have put us under siege. They want us to think we are alone. Flying the flag means others will know they are not alone. In the 2020 presidential election, we put up a Trump sign in our yard. Within a few days, there were four more on our block. And we live in very-liberal Northern Virginia that went 73 percent for Joe Biden. When you raise the flag, people know where to rally to.

Without a doubt, this could make things uneasy for some, but it will not threaten your job and your career.

Go further if you are so called and if you are concerned. For instance, take your kids out of public school. And let everyone, including the school, know why. Start a hybrid school out of your church. Start a lecture series at your church and invite local and statewide culture warriors to talk about their work.

Understand this. When you raise the flag, others will rally to it. They are waiting to know that others are like them.

Third, charge the sniper's nest.

This is not for the faint of heart and not for those who fear for their livelihood. This means making a public speech at the school board meeting. It means getting on the board of directors of a group fighting the LGBT agenda or for the unborn child. It means coming out in the open and understanding that the sniper will be firing at you. And you might get hit.

Let me tell you the story of a woman named Bethany Kozma. I mentioned her in one of the previous chapters. Bethany went from quiet and private to charging the sniper's nest in the span of a few years.

Bethany is married with young children and lives in Northern Virginia. She worked in the White House and in the Department of Homeland Security in the George W. Bush administration, but she did not work on controversial issues. Being an Evangelical, without a doubt, Bethany was pro-life and pro-family. People knew where she stood. She was not just private and quiet. She more than likely flew the flag. But then she made a speech at the Fairfax County School Board against the transgender policy that allowed boys to use the girls' restroom.

This speech would have been of no real consequence to her, except she was hired by President Trump to run the women's office of the U.S. Agency for International Development. Then came the snipers. This is what they said about her: "Bethany Kozma is a former George W. Bush administration staffer and an anti-transgender ideologue. She waged a fear-mongering campaign against her local school board, spreading the unsubstantiated claim that allowing students to use the bathroom consistent with their gender identity would put children at risk from sexual predators."[117] This is just one example of hundreds of attacks from leftist groups all over the world. All she did was make one two-minute speech.

What did Bethany do? She buckled in and doubled down. She became a leader in advancing the cause of life on behalf of the administration at the U.N. She fought against the LGBT agenda at USAID. They wanted to advance sexual-orientation and gender-identity international funding, and she fought it. She came under unmerciful attack from the LGBT cabal in the U.S. government. And she made a huge difference.

This is charging the sniper's nest. You may not be called to this. If you are, blessings upon you. If not, do things quietly and privately, or simply fly the flag. But do something.

The world is in such a mess; all you have to do to make it a better place is do something, do anything. As I say in the book, halos are hanging from the lowest branches of the trees. You don't even need to be on your tippy toes. Just reach up and grab one.

By all means, go to Mass every day if you can. Say the Rosary every day; say it with your family. Read Sacred Scripture every day. Find some spiritual reading. Find a spiritual director. Learn the Faith. Teach it to others, especially your children and your grandchildren. All of this is foundational.

Start today. Right now. There is so much to do and so few of us.

And remember, there has never been a finer time to be a faithful Catholic. Your descendants will say, "Weren't they amazing? How I wish I could have been there."

---

[117] "Bethany Kozma," Equity Forward, https://equityfwd.org/bethany -kozma.

About the Author

Austin Ruse is the president of C-Fam, a New York and Washington, D.C.–based research institute accredited to the U.N. Economic and Social Council and the Organization of American States. He is the author of three previous books, along with more than a thousand columns, essays, and articles. He lives in Northern Virginia with his wife, Cathy, and their daughters, Lucy and Gianna-Marie.

CRISIS Publications

Sophia Institute Press awards the privileged title "CRISIS Publications" to a select few of our books that address contemporary issues at the intersection of politics, culture, and the Church with clarity, cogency, and force and that are also destined to become all-time classics.

CRISIS Publications are *direct*, explaining their principles briefly, simply, and clearly to Catholics in the pews, on whom the future of the Church depends. The time for ambiguity or confusion is long past.

CRISIS Publications are *contemporary*, born of our own time and circumstances and intended to become significant statements in current debates, statements that serious Catholics cannot ignore, regardless of their prior views.

CRISIS Publications are *classical*, addressing themes and enunciating principles that are valid for all ages and cultures. Readers will turn to them time and again for guidance in other days and different circumstances.

CRISIS Publications are *spirited*, entering contemporary debates with gusto to clarify issues and demonstrate how those issues can be resolved in a way that enlivens souls and the Church.

We welcome engagement with our readers on current and future CRISIS Publications. Please pray that this imprint may help to resolve the crises embroiling our Church and society today.

A special thanks to our *Under Siege* launch team, who read this book before publication and helped us with promotion. Thank you for your time, input, and enthusiasm.

Jamie Adler, Brock Akers, Kathleen Alberque, Manuel Albert, Stephen Amoako, anonymous, Thomas Appel, Frank Apsey, Mauricio Arellano, Ramon Arguelles, Clemens Ast, Game Atfull, Jaime Banchs Pieretti, Veronica Bayer, Andrea Bayer, Deb Beck, Kay Behrenbruch, Edwin Benson, Les Beothy, Sylvie Bissonnette, Lisa Bjordal, Richard Bonomo, Esther Borja, Nancy Brady, Veronica Brandt, Kirkland Brush, Kevin Buckley, Gerald Burkepile, Jacek Cała, Michelle Cancinos, Maria Carrillo, Peter Carvill, Daniel Chan, Veysel Colak, Teresa Collett, Bernard Collins, Dr. Regina B. Colvin, James Cope, Christine Corea, Jakob Cornides, Peter Costea, Madeline Cottrell, Msgr. Thomas Crane, Robert Cropp, Martin Croxton, Solomon David, John Davis, Jose De Jesus, Caspar de Quay, John Dee, Anita Dekanic, Ma. Lizza Del Rosario, Fina Desouza, Roger Devaney, Kevin Devlin, Mo Dinverno, Loretta Dober, Dana Donia, George Doyle, Jonathan Dumlao, Tom Dunn, Alleen Eirich, Manfred Eliskases, Maria Kristina Entler, Mbachu Ernest, Laura Estrada, Michał Faflik, Fr David Fair, Leah Farish, M. Fernandes, Jana Ferner, Pam Fichter, Gail Finke, Paul Finlay, Mary Fitzgerald, William Fitzgibbons, Fredy Fong Olmos, Kathy Forck, Brian Ford, Sr. Alice S. Fulgencio, FMA, Chris and David Geddie, Peter Gichure, Daron Gifford, Camille Giglio, Ann Gillies, Fr. John Ginty, Mercedes González Amezúa, Sondra Gorius, David Grace, David Grace, Gerardina Guajardo, Jean-Eric Guindon, Fr. Matthew Habiger OSB, Chris Hanžek, Dee Harris, Andrew Harrod, Robert Harrold, Karin Heepen, Angela Heiter, Unbekannt Hennert, Wolfgang Hering, Peter Hodges, David M. Hodges, John Holecek, Aaron Hubert, Aaron Hubert, Kris Illenberger, Catholic Worker in the Vineyard, Lawrence Jardine, Warren Jensen, Dr. Godonou Jijoho Clement, Lawrence and Rhonda Jones, Fr. Kevin Joseph, Rommel Kapunan, M. Kaster, Clare Kedves, William Keegan, Maria Kelly, Sylvia Kendall, Maureen Keys, Richard Keys, Steven Kienlen, Mary King, Douglas Kingara, Bridget Kluesner, Gary Knight, Edward Kocourek, Diane Konicke, Dariusz Kowalczyk, Phil Kraemer, Mary Ann Kreitzer, Edward Krohn, Thomas Kuble, Sandra Kucharski,

Didier Lagae, Gabor Laszlo, Diane Lefebvre, Alejandro Limon, Clara Locher, JoAnn Lowe, Raúl Lucero, Kathleen Lund, Marcie Ly, Peter Lynch, Ken Madsen, Trevor Mahan, Thami Makhoba, Michal Makovník, Manuel Maldonado, Gregory Leo Phillip Sr. Manglitz, Christopher Manza, Marfynko Marfynko, José I. Marín, Kathryn (Kitty) McClellan, Barbara McNamara, Margaret McSheehy, Julia Meadows, Roy Mendoza, Kalie Meyers, Domenick Micillo, Weronika Mierzejewska, Michael J. Miller, Andrew Missler, Gabriel Mora, Matt Moran, Jim Morgan, Anthony Mulindwa, William Murat, Inkel Murguia, Madeleine Myers, Tobias Nauruki, Monica Navascues, Patrick Novecosky, Mara Nowak, Amy Nugent, Chris O'Brien, Frances O'Dair, Angela O'Neill, Doran Oancia, Lukáš Obšitník, Kerry Olvera, Michael Palid, Tracey Pinque, José Plasencia, Lilibeth Poot, Ernesto Pozas, James Prochaska, Ivan Prskalo, Antonio Puente, Jesus Qui Nieto, Francisco R. Mello, Miguel Raygoza, Dr. Jacob Reviriego, Martha Richardson, Kevin Rilott, Sylvia Rinelli, Lee Ann Rodgers, Jacqueline Rojes, Anthony and Georgette Romito, Myke Rosenthal-English, Marek Roszak, Michael Roth, Hannah Russo, Marcelo Santos, Jose Santos, Francois Savard, Stephen Scarallo, Mike Schafers, Julia Scott, George Seber, Amy Seymour, Barbara Sheddy, Patricia Sherk, Benjamin Simko, Jim Sinnerud, Ned Soyor, Karen Spaziante, Michael Spears, Thomas Spence, Paul Star, Joe and Karen Stein, Florence Suimin, Martin Szabo, David Talcott, C. S. Tey, Maria Therien Tout, Jolene Thompson, Eunice Tinant, Hugo Trindade, Kathleen Turbak, D. Turohan, Ant Vassallo, Lola Velarde, Rino Venturin, Margaret Voland, Damian von Stauffenberg, Vladimir Vorsic, Mariah Clare Webinger, Dcn. Andy Weiss, Eileen Weisslinger, Wesley Wensek, Alex Wesigye, Marc Wheat, Penny Wilke, David Wilson, James Wilson, Dave Wilson, Blair Witkowski, Donna Wright, Bruce Yocum, Louise Yoner, David Zarri, Paul Zeps